Business Architecture

The Missing Link in Strategy Formulation, Implementation and Execution

Pierre Hadaya

and

Bernard Gagnon

Montreal, Canada

Copy Editor: Zofia Laubitz

Cover Design: Alexandre Normand

ISBN: 978-0-9949319-0-0

Library and Archives Canada Cataloguing in Publication

Hadaya, Pierre, 1970-, author

    Business architecture : the missing link in strategy formulation, implementation and execution / Pierre Hadaya and Bernard Gagnon.

ISBN 978-0-9949319-0-0 (softcover)

    1. Strategic planning.   2. Organizational change.   I. Gagnon, Bernard, 1959-, author II. Title.

HD30.28.H33 2017   658.4'012   C2017-901193-6

To my wife and better half Isabelle, who guides and supports me in everything I do, and to my children, Janelle and Jérémie, who are my inspiration every day. I love you three more than words could ever express.

PH

To Lucie, Gabrielle and Simon for their love and invaluable support. I love you dearly.

BG

Table of Content

Chapter 1

Introduction

The corporate strategy revolution was launched after World War II when the word strategy began to creep into the corporate vocabulary with some regularity (Kiechel, 2010). Until then, the word had only been used by military theorists (Pascale, 1999). By the early 1980s, several strategic concepts, such as strengths, weaknesses, opportunities and threats (SWOT) analysis, five forces analysis and strategic positioning, had become common management language (Learned et al., 1969; Porter, 1979). Since then, a multitude of additional concepts (e.g., balanced scorecard, blue ocean strategy) have been introduced by researchers and practitioners to guide organizations in their strategic endeavors (Kaplan and Norton, 1996; Kim and Mauborgne, 2004). These strategic concepts are now so familiar and critical for organizations (Pascale, 1999) that strategy has become the framework organizations use most to understand what they are doing and determine what they should do (Kiechel, 2010) to create and sustain a competitive advantage (Collis and Rukstad, 2008; Porter, 1996).

Yet, despite all that has been learned since the advent of strategy in the corporate world, most organizations still struggle to succeed in their strategic endeavors (Charan and Colvin, 1999; Kiechel, 1982, 1984; The Economist Intelligence Unit Limited, 2013). This can be explained by the fact that, to create and sustain a competitive advantage, organizations must repeatedly overcome three difficult challenges. The first is to formulate a sound strategy. Surmounting this challenge requires that organizations deliberately choose to perform different activities from their rivals or to perform similar activities in different ways in order to deliver a unique mix of value that will give them a competitive advantage (Porter, 1996). This, in turn, demands that organizations excel at learning from their external and internal environments, formulating and analyzing alternative strategies and selecting the best one. The second challenge organizations face is to successfully implement their strategy. Surmounting this challenge requires that they become proficient at transforming themselves so they can execute the previously identified set of activities as desired. This, in turn, entails that they must excel at identifying all of the necessary transformations to the building blocks of which the organization is made up and grouping those transformations into projects that, once executed, will improve the organization's ability to execute its strategy. By building block, we mean any resource of which an organization is made up and which can be transformed (e.g., business processes, organizational units, IT systems, production facilities). The third challenge organizations face is to properly execute their strategy by performing the previously identified set of activities exactly as desired. This can only be done fully once all of the building block transformations required to implement the strategy (i.e., transform the organization) have been executed. By building block transformation, we mean a lasting change (i.e., acquisition/creation, modification or sale/retirement) made to an individual building block of the organization. Overcoming the challenges of formulating, implementing and executing a strategy is made particularly difficult by the limited knowledge organizations have of their constantly changing external and internal environments, and by people's natural resistance to change. Hence, to succeed, organizations must constantly motivate their troops to embrace continuous change, as well as monitor events, learn from new information and insights, and make the necessary adjustments to perfect the formulation, implementation and execution of their strategy.

Based on an extensive literature review and our own experience, we have identified 10 key issues organizations commonly face when trying to overcome the three challenges (Hunt, 2006; Kaplan and Norton, 1996, 2008; Khadem, 2008; Kotter, 1996; Mankins and Steele, 2005; Martin, 2010; Myers, 2001; Sull, 2007; Zagotta and Robinson, 2002). These 10 key issues and their consequences can be summarized as follows:

1. The feasibility analysis of the strategy alternatives being considered during the formulation of the strategy is not rigorous enough. Indeed, all too often, the main building block transformations that must be executed to implement each of these strategy alternatives are not identified, nor are their costs and time to completion estimated prior to the selection of the final strategy. As a result, the organization belatedly discovers that it does not have the means to implement the strategy it selected or that competitors with greater means are implementing a similar strategy faster than it can do so.

2. People do not know what they are supposed to do to implement the organization's strategy. Once the strategy is formulated, it is usually communicated to the members of the organization without the action plan needed to implement it. As a result, people do nothing or interpret the strategy in their own way and, despite their good intentions, do things that are at odds with each other and with the true intentions of the strategy.

3. The long-term financial plan and yearly budgets are not aligned with the strategy. In point of fact, the long-term financial plan and yearly budgets generally fail to correctly account for the size and timing of the revenues and expenses expected to occur as a result of the

implementation and execution of the strategy. Consequently, the speed at which the organization's financial performance should improve as a result of the execution of its strategy is often significantly overestimated. In addition, when stakeholders later realize that these unrealistic expectations cannot be met, they lose confidence in the strategy and scale down their efforts to implement and execute it.

4. The transformation projects[1] needed to implement the strategy are poorly identified and selected. Indeed, middle managers, who are generally responsible for proposing transformation projects and building the business cases for these projects, are often reluctant, for political and other reasons, to propose projects that will have an impact on functional areas other than their own. To make matters worse, these middle managers are often inclined to propose projects intended to alleviate local problems rather than to implement the strategy. As a result, many transformation projects that would contribute the most to the implementation of the strategy are never proposed.

5. People focus too much on the short term. Once the strategy has been formulated, people tend to forget all about it and focus on short-term issues and financial benefits. Consequently, the implementation of the strategy is constantly delayed and important opportunities are missed.

6. Priorities proliferate. In general, priorities are not clearly set and matched to the organization's capacity to transform itself. Thus, too many transformation projects are launched at once, and activities and projects that are no longer needed are not halted.

---

[1] By *transformation project*, we mean the actual execution of a coherent set of building block transformations that once executed will improve the organization's ability to execute its strategy.

7. The transformation projects are executed in a sub-optimal order. In fact, a strategy is usually implemented more or less in the order in which the projects are proposed, without taking in consideration the dependencies between them. As a result, building block transformations cost more and take more time than they should because rework is required. In addition, potential synergies, which better sequencing could have provided, are lost.

8. The required IT system transformations are difficult to identify and justify. Without a global picture of the business transformations that must be made to execute the strategy, it is difficult to properly identify and justify all of the IT system transformations that are needed. As a result, IT systems are not transformed as they should be during the implementation of the strategy. Instead, they become a hindrance to its execution.

9. The budgeting process impairs the implementation of the strategy. Indeed, the budgeting process often lacks the agility required to optimize the use of available resources and transform the organization effectively and efficiently. The result is that the strategy takes longer to implement than it should and transformation capacity is wasted along the way.

10. There is a lack of leadership. Executives and other leaders make little effort to communicate the strategy, motivate and get buy-in and commitment from all stakeholders[2] to implement and execute the strategy. In addition, executives and other leaders do not spend enough time monitoring events, learning from new information and insights, and making the necessary adjustments to the formulation, implementation and execution of the strategy. As a result, members of the organization resist change, some issues are never resolved and opportunities are missed.

---

[2] By stakeholder, we mean any person or group with an interest or concern in the transformation of the organization. This includes all members of the organization as well as business partners that will be impacted by the transformation of the organization.

Business Architecture: The Missing Link

Practitioners and researchers have proposed a number of best practices that organizations can use to alleviate the 10 key issues identified above that hinder most strategic endeavors (Coon and Wolf, 2005; Hunt, 2006; Kaplan and Norton, 1996, 2005, 2008; Khadem, 2008; Kotter, 1996, 2002; Mankins and Steele, 2005; Martin, 2010; Myers, 2001; Sull, 2007; Zagotta and Robinson, 2002). Despite their importance, these best practices do not suffice to resolve the issues entirely. Our professional experience tells us that most organizations are still missing three key components to surmount the strategy formulation, implementation and execution challenges more easily:

1. A target business architecture (TBA) that defines how the organization must function in the future to be able to execute its strategy in full. By "execute its strategy in full," we mean that the organization fully delivers the unique mix of value at the heart of its strategy and that its building blocks have been transformed accordingly.

2. A transformation plan (TP), which identifies and sequences the transformation projects that must be executed during the next three to five years in order to improve the organization's ability to execute its strategy.

3. An internal business architecture practice that is responsible for architecting the TBA and elaborating the TP, and that contributes to other strategy formulation, implementation and execution activities the organization must master to create and maintain a competitive advantage for itself. By architecting the TBA, we mean designing, modeling and documenting the TBA.

The sum of these three components makes up what we call business architecture – the missing link in strategy formulation, implementation and execution. The following subsections further describe each of these three business architecture components, together with their respective purpose, and explain the benefits business architecture can provide for an organization.

The Target Business Architecture

The TBA is a "blueprint" that defines how the organization must function in the future to be able to execute its strategy in full. To do so, the TBA first identifies[3] the business capabilities, business functions, business processes, organizational units, know-how assets, information assets and brands that will be needed for this purpose[4], and defines the desired key features of these business architecture building blocks. Second, the TBA identifies the natural resource deposits and most important technology assets that will be needed but does not define their key features including the functioning of the technology assets. Third, the TBA identifies and defines the desired key features of the relationships the business architecture building blocks must have with one another and with the natural resource deposit and main technology asset building blocks. Architecting the TBA is a great opportunity for stakeholders to think holistically about how to improve the functioning of their organization.

The TBA is a subset of the target enterprise architecture (TEA). In addition to defining how the organization must function in the future to be able to execute its strategy in full, the TEA defines how the organization's technology assets must function for this purpose. The TEA identifies, and defines the desired key features of, all the enterprise architecture building blocks[5] (i.e., capabilities, functions, processes, organizational units, know-how assets, information assets, brands as well as natural resource deposits and technology assets) and of the relationships that all these enterprise architecture building blocks will have to have with one another. As shown in Figure 1.1, the TEA includes the TBA and possibly a number of target technology architectures (TTAs), such as the target IT enterprise architecture (TITEA) and the target manufacturing technology architecture,

---

[3] The identification of a building block includes a brief description of the same.

[4] To lighten the text throughout the book, we will minimize the use of the word "business" when talking about business capabilities, business functions and business processes by simply referring to them as capabilities, functions and processes.

[5] When not otherwise indicated, we use the words "building blocks" to mean "enterprise architecture building blocks" throughout the remainder of this book.

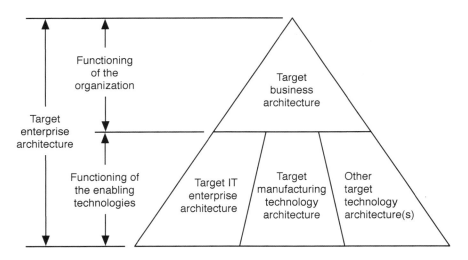

Figure 1.1: The components of a target enterprise
architecture and their relationships

which respectively define how the information systems and manufacturing technologies must function in the future. Together, the TBA and the TTAs must form a coherent whole. For this reason, they should be architected in parallel. Although some organizations' TEAs only include a TBA and a TITEA, TEAs may need to include other TTAs. The types of TTAs needed vary according to the mission of the organization. For example, the TEA of a parcel delivery company, such as UPS, needs to include a target parcel delivery technology architecture that defines how its sorting centers, the sorting technologies in these centers and its transport technologies (e.g., airplanes, trucks) must be used in the future to efficiently pick up parcels from its customers and deliver them at their final destination.

It is important to mention here that architecting the TBA and the TEA requires the modeling of the current business architecture (CBA) and of the current enterprise architecture (CEA) respectively to facilitate the identification of the enterprise architecture building blocks that must be leveraged and those that should be transformed during the implementation of the strategy.

The Transformation Plan

A TP identifies and sequences the transformation projects that the organization must execute to implement parts or all of its TEA. It is based on a comparison between the CEA and TEA to identify the building block transformations that must be executed to improve the organization's ability to execute its strategy. Because it can take a decade or more for an organization to implement its TEA in full and because things always change along the way, at any point in time the TP should cover only the next three to five years of the strategy implementation. The elaboration of the TP should account for the need to continuously improve the organization's financial performance; the extended organization's capacity and readiness to transform itself; the need to build and maintain momentum throughout the implementation of the strategy; and the strategic importance, interdependence, benefits, costs, elapsed time to completion, assumptions and risks associated with each building block transformation. The purpose of the TP is to break the transformation of the organization down into manageable projects and to work out the order in which these projects should be executed to enable the organization to progressively improve its financial performance throughout the implementation and execution of its strategy.

The Business Architecture Practice

The idea of a business architecture practice originates from the convergence of work done by multiple professional practices such as strategic planning, organizational design, business process improvement, knowledge management, business continuity planning and IT enterprise architecture. Each of these professional practices has been independently developing expertise in modeling and architecting certain building blocks of the current and target functioning of the organization. For example, strategists use capabilities and functions (e.g., Porter value chain), while organizational design specialists use functions and organizational structures to improve their organization's competitiveness in their own way. By relying on a business architecture practice to design and/or model all of the business architecture building blocks, organizations can ensure that the models they produce of the current and target states of their functioning are more coherent and serve them better as a whole. Obviously, members of the business architecture practice (i.e., business architects) need to work in close collaboration with members of other professional practices to make sure that their models meet the needs of these other professionals.

To explain the purpose of a business architecture practice and of the related business architect profession in more detail, we rely on the seven complementary groups of activities that organizations must master to overcome the challenges of formulating, implementing and executing a strategy (Figure 1.2). Each of these groups includes only the activities that are specific to that group's purpose. The Engage and Govern group of activities serves to motivate and get buy-in from all stakeholders and to remove barriers to the formulation, implementation and execution of the strategy. It also serves to monitor events and the progress of the building block transformations, learn from new information and insights, and make the necessary adjustments to the formulation, implementation and execution of the strategy. The purpose of the Formulate the Strategy group of activities is specifically to learn from the external and internal environments, formulate and analyze strategy alternatives, and select the best one. The purpose of the Architect the TBA and Architect the TTAs groups of activities is to design, model and document the TBA and the TTAs, respectively. The purpose of the Elaborate the TP group of activities is to identify, select and sequence the transformation projects. The purpose of the Execute the TP group of activities is to execute the transformation projects included in the TP so the organization can implement parts or all of its TEA. The Architect the TBA, Architect the TTAs, Elaborate the TP and Execute the TP groups of activities are specific to strategy implementation. These four groups are required to identify the necessary building block transformations and sequence and execute them in an effective, efficient and timely manner. The

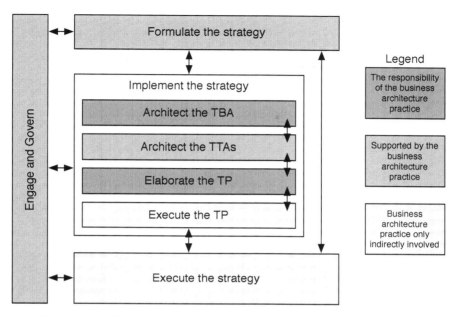

Figure 1.2: The seven groups of activities required to formulate, implement and execute a strategy

organization's operating activities (e.g., production, procurement, marketing, sales and customer service) are bundled together in what we call the Execute the Strategy group of activities since these are the only activities that can truly execute the organization's strategy. The double arrows in Figure 1.2 identify the interactions between the seven groups of activities. For example, the activities of the Engage and Govern group are performed in combination with the strategy formulation, implementation and execution activities. The activities of the Execute the Strategy group also interact directly with the activities of the Formulate the Strategy group because organizations are usually able to start executing their strategy to some degree without executing any building block transformations beforehand.

We must emphasize that the Formulate the Strategy, Architect the TBA, Architect the TTAs and Elaborate the TP groups of activities must be performed iteratively. There are three reasons for this. First, the strategy,

TBA, TTAs and TP should be revisited regularly to account for changing market conditions, competitors' strategic moves, new technologies and other new information, insights and ideas gained by the organization. Second, the effort of architecting the TBA and the TTAs must be divided into a series of successive increments that each focus on a distinct set of priorities. This is necessary because, although it can take many years to completely architect a TBA and TTAs, an organization cannot wait until these target architectures are completed before it begins implementing its strategy. Third, because the TBA and the TTAs must be built incrementally, the TP must also be elaborated incrementally.

The primary purpose of a business architecture practice is to architect the TBA and elaborate the TP (activity groups highlighted in dark gray in Figure 1.2). Business architects should devise these two plans in close collaboration with executives, middle managers, subject matter experts and other professionals across the organization. They should act as catalysts in gathering the best building block transformation ideas throughout the organization and merging them into a coherent whole that is aligned with the strategy. The secondary purpose of a business architecture practice is to contribute to the Formulate the Strategy, Architect the TTAs and Engage and Govern groups of activities (activity groups shown in medium gray in Figure 1.2). For example, business architects should help strategists analyze the feasibility of the strategy alternatives. They should also collaborate with IT and other technology architects in architecting their respective TTAs. Conversely, these professionals should support business architects in architecting the TBA and elaborating the TP. In addition, business architects should help executives engage their people in the transformation of the organization and contribute to the governance of this transformation. Note that business architects do not contribute directly to the execution of the TP or of the strategy; instead, they contribute to them through the Engage and Govern group of activities (activity groups shown in light gray in Figure 1.2).

Integrating Business Architecture into the Organization

According to Kaplan and Norton (2008, p. 7-8), organizations need to have a *"comprehensive and integrated management system that links strategy formulation and planning with operational execution"* to be able to successfully formulate, implement and execute their strategy. We call this management system the Formulate and Align to Strategy (**FAS**) business capability.

The literature suggests many best practices that organizations should implement into their FAS capability. However, if business architecture is not integrated into it, the FAS capability is impaired and cannot fully alleviate the 10 key issues identified above. The reverse is also true. To generate its full benefits, business architecture must be well integrated into the organization's FAS capability. The purpose of the resulting business-architecture-enabled FAS (**baeFAS**) capability is to perform all of the Engage and Govern, Formulate the Strategy and Implement the Strategy groups of activities identified above. This critical capability should include all of the sub-capabilities, functions, processes, organizational units, know-how assets, information assets and technology assets (information systems in this case) needed to enable the organization to successfully overcome the challenges of formulating and implementing its strategy as well as overseeing (i.e., monitoring and making decisions that pertain to) the formulation, implementation and execution of its strategy. The baeFAS capability ensures that all of the organization's other capabilities are aligned to its strategy. The baeFAS does not actually execute the organization's strategy since it can only be truly executed by core capabilities such as Design Products, Market and Sell Products and Services, and Manufacture Products.

To reap the full benefits of their baeFAS capability, organizations must also integrate its activities with other long-term planning activities such as long-term financial planning and product development planning[6]. The outputs of all of these long-term planning activities (see Figure 1.3) should be key inputs into the organization's short-term planning activities (12- to 18-month outlooks). For example, the estimated costs and benefits of the transformation projects included in the TP should be used as inputs to draft the short-term financial plan (i.e., budget or rolling financial forecast). The sales and operations plans should also account for new production capacity made available by the completion of the projects included in the TP.

Benefits

When it is well integrated into an organization's FAS capability and long-term planning activities, and used in combination with best practices identified by other authors, business architecture (i.e., TBA, TP and the business architecture practice) can enable the organization to significantly alleviate, and in some cases completely resolve, each of the 10 key issues identified above that commonly make it difficult to formulate, implement and execute a strategy:

1. By outlining the TBA and TP related to each strategy alternative being considered (i.e., identifying the main building block transformations required, creating high-level estimates of their costs and benefits and drafting a preliminary roadmap for the execution of these transformations), business architects can provide essential information for analyzing the feasibility of these strategy alternatives.

2. By communicating the TBA and TP to its members, in addition to the strategy, the organization can give its stakeholders a clear understanding of what building block transformations must be done to implement the strategy.

---

[6] Note that, since some industries have short product development cycles, product development planning activities are sometimes part of the short-term planning cycle.

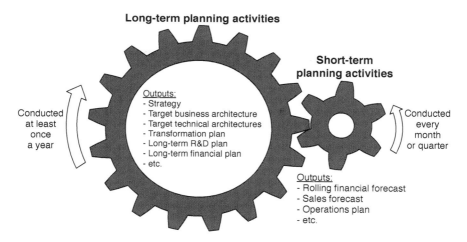

Figure 1.3: Activities in an organization's long-term
and short-term planning cycles

3. By leveraging the investment and benefit forecast information built into the TP, the organization can ensure that the long-term and short-term financial plans are better aligned with the strategy.

4. By gathering the best building block transformation ideas throughout the organization, including those whose impacts span multiple functional areas, and by merging them in a coherent set, business architects can architect a TBA and elaborate a TP that is truly designed to implement the strategy.

5. By conducting Engage and Govern activities to align people's priorities with those set in the TP, the organization can alleviate people's natural tendency to focus on short-term issues and, in so doing, ensure that the strategy is implemented at the desired pace.

6. By rigorously accounting for the extended organization's capacity to transform itself, a sound TP can help launch the right projects at the right time, stop projects that are no longer needed, and thus avoid priority proliferation.

7. By accounting for the interdependencies between transformation projects and the benefits these projects will provide to the organization, a sound TP can sequence projects in an order that will meet the need to provide steadily increasing benefits to the organization while minimizing rework and the associated costs and delays.

8. By providing a clear description of how the organization must function in the future to be able to execute its strategy in full, the TBA makes it easier for IT enterprise architects to define how the IT systems will have to be transformed to support this functioning.

9. By identifying the benefits and resource requirements (e.g., financial, human and technology assets) of each transformation project, as well as the extended organization's readiness and capacity to transform itself, the TP, used in tandem with a rolling financial forecast, can provide the agility the project funding process requires to optimize the use of resources available for the implementation of the strategy.

10. By contributing to the Engage and Govern activities (e.g., communicating the TBA and the TP, and learning from events and adapting the TBA and TP), business architects can provide some of the leadership required to successfully overcome the challenges of formulating, implementing and executing a strategy.

In essence, to adopt business architecture is to embrace the age-old adage Festina lente, which means that *"activities should be performed with a proper balance of urgency and diligence [and that] if tasks are overly rushed, mistakes are made and good long-term results are not achieved"* (Wikipedia contributors, n.d.). By leveraging business architecture, organizations can more effectively and efficiently transform themselves to deliver the unique mix of value at the heart of their strategy. Business architecture is a holistic approach, which offers organizations a proper balance of urgency and diligence to formulate and implement their strategy. It enables organizations to select and optimize the building block transformations they plan to execute based on the strategic importance, benefits, costs, interdependences, time to completion and risks of each transformation while carefully considering the synergies and other ramifications these transformations can have throughout the organization. By helping organizations make judicious choices before any significant amount of time and money has been invested, business architecture facilitates the effective and efficient transformation of the organization and mitigates the risk of belatedly discovering that the wrong building block transformations have been done, that the right building block transformations have been done incorrectly, or that transformations have been done in the wrong order.

Book Structure

The goal of this book is to describe what business architecture is; how it can help surmount the challenge of formulating, implementing and executing an organization's strategy; and how to build and exploit a baeFAS capability. To achieve this goal, we rely on six chapters. Chapters 2 to 5 describe how business architects can contribute to the different activity groups that an organization should rely upon to successfully overcome the challenges of formulating, implementing and executing a strategy. Chapter 2 describes how business architects can contribute to the formulation of their organization's strategy. Before describing these contributions, the chapter summarizes the fundamental knowledge every business architect should have, namely what a strategy is and what a strategic plan is. Chapter 3 demystifies the core concepts that correspond to the nine types of "enterprise architecture building blocks" used to define how the organization must function in the future to be able to execute its strategy in full and describes how business architects should go about architecting the TBA using these concepts. Chapter 4 describes the key characteristics and components of a sound

TP and proposes a methodology to elaborate one. Chapter 5 describes the Engage and Govern activities that are relevant to the work of business architects and explains how business architects can contribute to each one. Chapter 6 presents our reference architecture for the baeFAS capability, which puts together all of the concepts described in the previous chapters. It presents the integrated set of sub-capabilities, functions, roles, processes, organizational units, decision rights, know-how assets, information assets and information system assets which should be at the heart of this capability. It also describes how this capability should function and highlights how business architects should contribute to it. Finally, Chapter 7 lays out a leadership agenda for organizations wishing to put business architecture into practice and adopt the frameworks and methodologies set out in the previous chapters.

Before Continuing

This book was written for readers who want an in-depth understanding of what business architecture is; how it can help surmount the challenge of formulating, implementing and executing an organization's strategy; and how to apply the practice of business architecture to build and exploit a baeFAS capability. However, this book can also be useful to readers who want only a high-level understanding of these issues. These readers could skip most of Chapters 3 and 4. The introductions to these two chapters indicate which sections members of this particular audience might want to read.

References

Charan, R. and Colvin, G. (1999) Why CEOs Fail. *Fortune*, 139(12), 68-78.

Collis, D.J., and Rukstad, M.G. (2008) Can You Say What Your Strategy Is? *Harvard Business Review*, April, 82-90.

Coon, B., and Wolf, S. (2005) The Alchemy of Strategy Execution. *Employment Relations Today*, 32(3), 19-30.

Hunt, S. (2006) *Building Finance and Performance Management Mastery with Superior Budgeting and Forecasting Capabilities*. Accenture.

Kaplan, R.S., and Norton, D.P. (1996) *The Balanced Scorecard: Translating Strategy into Action*. Harvard Business Publishing, Boston.

Kaplan, R.S., and Norton, D.P. (2005) The Office of Strategy Management. *Harvard Business Review*, 83(10), 72-80.

Kaplan, R.S., and Norton, D.P. (2008) *The Execution Premium: Linking Strategy to Operations for Competitive Advantage*. Harvard Business Publishing, Boston.

Kiechel, W. (1982) Corporate Strategists Under Fire. *Fortune*, December, 106(13), 34-39.

Kiechel, W. (1984). Sniping at Strategic Planning. *Planning Review*, May, 8-11.

Kiechel, W. III. (2010) The Lords of Strategy, *The Secret Intellectual History of the New Corporate World*. Harvard Business Publishing, Boston.

Khadem, R. (2008) Alignment and Follow-Up: Steps to Strategy Execution. *Journal of Business Strategy*, 29(6), 29-35.

Kim, W.C., and Mauborgne, R. (2005) *Blue Ocean Strategy: How to Create Uncontested Market Space and Make Competition Irrelevant*. Harvard Business Publishing, Boston.

Kotter, J. P. (1996) *Leading Change*. Harvard Business Publishing, Boston.

Kotter, J. P. (2002) *The Heart of change: Real-Life Stories of How People Change Their Organizations*. Harvard Business Publishing, Boston.

Learned, E.P., Christiansen, C.R., Andrews, K., and Guth, W.D. (1969). *Business Policy, Text and Cases*. Richard D. Irwin, Homewood, Ill.

Mankins, M.C., and Steele, R. (2005) Turning Great Strategy into Great Performance. *Harvard Business Review*, 83(7/8), 64-72.

Martin, R. (2010) The Execution Trap. *Harvard Business Review*, 83(7/8), 64-72.

Myers, R. (2001) Budgets on a Roll: Recalculating a Business's Outlook Several Times a Year. *Journal of Accountancy*, 192(6), 41-46.

Pascale, R.T. (1999) Surfing the Edge of Chaos. *Sloan Management Review*, 40(3), 83-94.

Porter, M.E. (1979) How Competitive Forces Shape Strategy. *Harvard Business Review*, 57(2), 137-145.

Porter, M.E. (1996) What Is Strategy? *Harvard Business Review*, November-December, 61-78.

Sull, D.N. (2007) Closing the Gap Between Strategy and Execution. *MIT Sloan Management Review*, 48(4), 30-38.

The Economist Intelligence Unit Limited (2013) *Why Good Strategies Fail : Lessons from the C-Suite*.

Wikipedia contributors (2016) Festina Lente. (n.d.) In *Wikipedia, The Free Encyclopedia*. Retrieved Wikimedia Foundation, [WWW document] https://en.wikipedia.org/wiki/Festina_lente (accessed August 14, 2016).

Zagotta, R., and Robinson, D. (2002) Keys to Successful Strategy Execution. *Journal of Business Strategy*, 23(1), 30-34.

Chapter 2

Contributing to Strategy Formulation

In order to be able to contribute to the formulation of the strategy of their organization and use it as the starting point for their business architecture efforts, business architects must understand what a strategy is and how it is formulated and codified. They must also be familiar with the other components of a strategic plan that must first be outlined to support the formulation of a strategy, and later architected in detail to support its implementation and execution. The objective of this chapter is to provide a concise introduction to these topics. The first section describes what a strategy is and proposes the Strategic Plan Framework designed to help organizations formulate, implement and execute their strategy. The second section describes the Formulate the Strategy group of activities and explains how business architects can contribute to each one. The third and last section presents key templates that strategists and business architects can use to codify their organization's strategy, together with key elements of the corresponding long-term research and development (R&D) plan, target enterprise architecture (TEA) and transformation plan (TP).

The Strategic Plan Framework

Strategy is defined in many ways in the business literature. Our definition of the term is based on the concept of strategic positioning proposed by Michael Porter (1996), as well as the works of several other eminent authors in the field including Kaplan and Norton (2004) and Collis and Rukstad (2008). We define strategy as follows:

> A market position that an organization adopts to create a unique mix of value for its owners, customers, partners and employees while enabling it to set itself apart from its current and potential competitors in a positive way.

This unique and valuable position is defined using four complementary components: values, mission, vision and stakeholder value propositions. Each component defines a particular set of position attributes; together, they describe how the organization wants to behave in the future.

Based on the above definition of strategy, we propose the Strategic Plan Framework shown in Figure 2.1. This framework has nine components. The four components at the top of the figure (i.e., values, mission, vision, and stakeholder value propositions) define the organization's complete strategy, while the five supporting components at the bottom of the figure (i.e., long-term R&D plan, TEA, TP, long-term financial plan, and objectives) are used to guide the implementation of the strategy and evaluate the success of both its implementation and execution. With its modular design, this framework helps to break the complex job of formulating and maintaining a strategic plan down into manageable components.

Because each component of the Strategic Plan Framework should flow from those above it, the components of the framework should be defined from top to bottom to ensure that they form a coherent whole. The four strategy components of the framework should be completely defined during the Strategy Formulation process, while the five supporting components should only be outlined during strategy formulation and then detailed and refined during strategy implementation and execution.

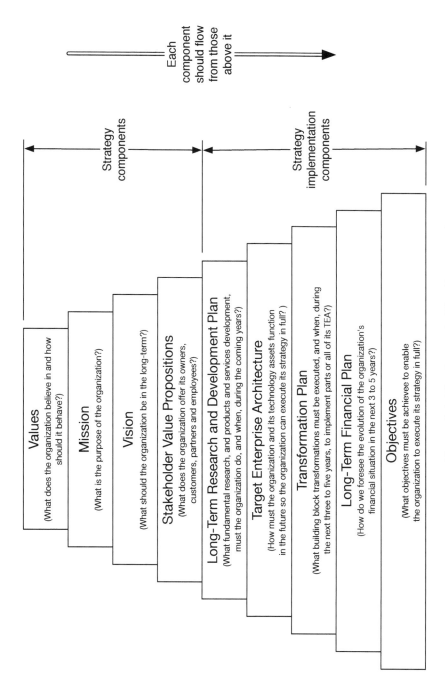

Figure 2.1: The Strategic Plan Framework

The following two subsections describe each of the components of the Strategic Plan Framework and the relationships that exist between the various concepts. The last subsection discusses the number of strategic plans required by different types of multi-business-unit organizations.

The Strategy Components

Values

Values are principles or standards of behavior that are important to the organization. They position the organization by representing what it believes in and how it wishes to behave (Collis and Rukstad, 2008). Values must come first as they influence the organization's choice of mission, vision and stakeholders value propositions. For example, a group of people may start a charity because they place a high value on helping others. Values are principles that simultaneously guide and constrain the actions of the organization and its members. They should be long-lived – some companies have had the same values for decades – and held dear by members of the organization, especially the executives whose actions must be traceable to these values. For example, an organization could have the following values:

- Innovation: We are continually improving and reinventing our products to keep up with trends and address the changing needs of our customers.

- Teamwork: Collaboration is our keystone. We believe strongly that the whole is greater than the sum of its parts.

- Excellence: We strive for excellence in everything that we do.

- Customer satisfaction: Satisfied customers are essential to our success.

- Good corporate citizenship: We provide a safe workplace, protect the environment and engage in philanthropy.

Mission

The mission is an actionable statement that identifies the purpose of the organization. It positions the organization, implicitly or explicitly, in one or more industries and specifies what it aims to do within these industries. Examples of well-formulated mission statements include:

- *"To give ordinary people the chance to buy the same things as rich people"* (Walmart)

- *"To solve unsolved problems innovatively"* (3M)

Vision

The vision is a concise inspirational statement that defines the organization's desired long-term state. It represents a goal, *"an aim or desired result"* (*New Oxford American Dictionary*).

Examples of properly formulated vision statements are:

- *"Become $125 billion company by year 2000"* (Walmart, 1990)

- *"Become the dominant player in commercial aircraft and bring the world into the jet age"* (Boeing, 1950)

Stakeholder Value Propositions

The stakeholder value propositions component of the Strategic Plan Framework comprises four complementary sub-components: (1) owner value proposition; (2) customer value proposition; (3) partner value proposition; and (4) employee value proposition. These sub-components are key in creating a unique and valuable strategic position that will enable an organization to set itself apart from its competitors in a positive way.

First, the owner value proposition describes the value the organization wants to provide for its owners to justify their participation in its ownership. This value proposition is defined using four position attributes, presented below with examples of questions that the organization needs to answer to define them:

- Returns: What financial return should the owners expect?

- Growth: What revenue growth should the owners expect?

- Risk: What level of risk should the owners be willing to accept?

- Corporate citizenship: What is the organization's position with regard to protecting the environment and engaging in philanthropy?

The customer value proposition describes:

> the unique mix of product and services attributes, customer relations, and corporate image that a company wants to offer. It defines how the organization will differentiate itself from competitors to attract, retain and deepen relationships with targeted customers (Kaplan and Norton, 2000, p. 53).

According to Kaplan and Norton (2004), the customer value proposition is defined using the following eight position attributes:

- Price/Cost: At what price should the organization's products/services be sold to customers?

- Availability: How easy should it be for customers to find and buy the organization's products/services? Should the products always be in stock and in sufficient quantity? How long should it take for customers to receive the products/services once they purchase them? In what geographic regions will the products/service be available?

- Quality: Product/service quality can take many forms. How easy should it be to use the product/service? How reliable should the product/service be? What is the acceptable defect rate? How much time and effort will the customer need to invest to get the product/ service working at a fully functional level?

- Selection: How broad should the organization's product and service offerings be?

- Functionality: How functionally rich should the products/services be?

- Service: How good should the pre- and post-sale services provided by the organization be? How good is the product/service training? Do customers need to bring the products in for service or does the organization provide service on site (only for products)? How easy is it for customers to find a service center?

- Partnership[1]: How can the organization improve customer relationships? How can the organization help customers maximize the benefits they get from the products/services?

- Image: How exclusive should the brand be? How strong should the brand-quality association be? How does owning or using products and services of the brand influence the customer's own image?

Empirical research has identified four successful generic customer value propositions that organizations can choose from to gain a competitive advantage (Hax, Wilde and Thurow, 2001; Kim and Mauborgne, 2005; Porter, 1980; Treacy and Wiersema, 1995): operational excellence, customer intimacy, product/service leadership, and value innovation[2]. Organizations that pursue operational excellence focus on minimizing the product/service cost of ownership for customers. They excel at such things as competitive pricing, product quality and selection, and speedy delivery. Organizations pursuing customer intimacy (i.e., complete solution providers) focus on developing high-quality relationships with customers in order to discover and meet all of their needs. Organizations that seek product/service leadership concentrate on the functionalities and performance of their products and services (Treacy and Wiersema, 1995). Finally, value innovation organizations create new markets ("blue oceans") by introducing something so innovative that they will have no direct competitors in this new market space for some time (Kim and Mauborgne, 2005). Apple's introduction of the iPad in 2010 was an example of a value innovation strategy.

---

[1]   This position attribute refers only to partnerships with customers.

[2]   Although some authors refer to these generic value propositions as generic strategies, they do not constitute full strategies in our framework.

It is important to note here that some organizations may have two or more very important customer groups to whom they offer very different, but synergistic, value propositions. For example, Google gives the general public free access to its Internet search engine. These searches generate traffic on websites, and this attracts advertisers willing to pay a fee to Google. When such synergistic customer value propositions exist, it is best to define each customer value proposition separately.

The partner value proposition describes the value the organization provides to its partners (e.g., suppliers, distributors, wholesalers, complementors[3]) – those collaborators that contribute to the organization's customer value proposition – to justify the investments (in time and money) they must make to build and maintain a relationship with the organization. This value proposition is defined using four position attributes:

- Financial: What sales growth, cost reductions, and net margin increase should the partners get in return for building and maintaining a relationship with the organization?

- Collaboration: What level of collaboration in terms of information sharing, decision synchronization and incentive alignment should partners expect (Simatupang and Sridharan, 2005)?

- Investments: What level of investment in terms of specific assets (e.g., plant, machinery, IT), skill development, and support (e.g., marketing, sales) should the partners expect from the organization (Maheshwari, Kumar and Kumar, 2006)?

- Reputation: What benefits can partners reap from the organization's track record, image, trustworthiness, commitment and ability to

---

[3] *"A player is your complementor if your customers value your product more when they have the other player's product than when they have your product alone"* (Brandenburger and Nalebuff, 1997; p. 18).

differentiate itself from its competitors in terms of operational excellence, customer intimacy or product leadership?

Minchington (2010) defines the employee value proposition as a set of associations and offerings provided by the organization in return for its employees' work, skills, capabilities and experiences. This value proposition is defined using six position attributes (including the five proposed by Sibson Consulting, 2014):

- Compensation: What income (including base salary, incentives, cash recognition, and premium pay) should employees expect to receive for their work?

- Benefits: What indirect compensation (including health and retirement benefits and time off) should employees expect to receive for their work?

- Work content: What level of variety, challenge, autonomy and feedback should employees expect when doing their work?

- Career: What long-term opportunities in terms of advancement, personal growth, training and employment security should employees expect to receive for their work?

- Affiliation: What organizational commitment and trust, and work environment should employees expect to receive for their work?

- Health and safety: What health and security protection should employees expect from their organization?

The Strategy Implementation Components

The purpose of the next five components of the Strategic Plan Framework is to support the implementation and execution of the strategy.

Long-term Research and Development Plan

The long-term R&D plan defines what fundamental research, and what products and services development, the organization wants to do, and when, in the coming years. It also identifies the investments that will be needed to execute the plan. The breadth (i.e., number of years) and depth (e.g., products/services versus product/service lines) needed for this plan vary from one industry to the next. For example, an aerospace company may need to define each of the aircraft models (i.e., products) it will develop during the next decade, or more, while a consumer electronics company may only need to define the number of new products it wants to develop and market during the next three years in each of its product lines.

Target Enterprise Architecture

The TEA is a plan that defines how the organization must function in the future to be able to execute its strategy in full and how the organization's technology assets must function for this purpose. To do so, the TEA identifies, and defines the desired key features, of all the enterprise architecture building blocks (i.e., business capabilities, business functions, business processes, organizational units, know-how assets, information assets, brands, natural resource deposits and technology assets) and the relationships that all of these enterprise architecture building blocks must have with one another. The TEA includes the target business architecture (TBA), the target IT enterprise architecture (TITEA) and possibly other target technology architectures (TTAs) (e.g., the target manufacturing technology architecture).

Transformation Plan

The TP identifies and sequences the transformation projects that the organization must execute during the next three to five years to implement parts or all of its TEA. To do so, the TP identifies, based on a comparison between the current state and the TEA (i.e., TBA and TTAs), the building block transformations[4] that must be executed during the next three to five years to implement parts or all of the TEA and groups them

---

[4]   By building block transformation, we mean a lasting change made to a building block of the organization.

into projects formulated to deliver coherent and operative results. The TP also identifies project interdependencies, risks, assumptions, and estimated efforts, costs and benefits.

Long-Term Financial Plan

The long-term financial plan is a long-term forecast of the evolution of the organization's financial position. It describes the organization's financial goals for the next three to five years, when those goals are to be achieved, and the investments that will be needed to reach them. The long-term financial plan includes an income statement, a balance sheet, and a cash flow statement. It must be closely linked to the strategy (Mankins and Steele, 2005). In addition, it must reflect the schedule of R&D and transformation projects that are planned to be executed and the investments required to complete them, as well as the financial benefits each of these projects is expected to provide to the organization. Finally, it must provide insight into the organization's capacity to conduct its regular business activities. The long-term financial plan is generally updated once a year to forecast revenues and expenditures, using assumptions about economic conditions, future spending and investment scenarios, and other salient variables.

Objectives

As mentioned above, goals are aims or desired results. Goals can be broadly classified into two groups: transformation goals that require transformations to be attained (e.g., build a new factory to increase production) and continuance goals that do not require transformations to be attained as they relate to things the organization already does well and wants to continue doing the same way.

Objectives are measurable, quantified goals with an associated timeframe. For example, a transformation goal may be to "deliver products on time," whereas the corresponding transformation objective may be to "have 99.8% of products delivered on-time by 2019." An objective relies on a metric, which in this case is the percentage of products delivered on time. Transformation and continuance objectives should be set for each element of the other seven components of the strategic plan framework.

To achieve a transformation objective, an organization may also need to define intermediate objectives, called targets, which identify the desired progress towards the attainment of the objective at different time points along the way. The last target in a series corresponds to the objective to be attained. For example, if the current percentage of on-time product deliveries is 97.3% and the transformation objective is to have 99.8% of products delivered on-time by 2019, then the targets in the strategic plan may be 98.5% by the end of 2017 and 99.3% by the end of 2018. Objectives and targets are used to compare the actual level to the desired level of attainment of the organization's goals.

Realistic objectives and targets can only be set once all building block transformations required for their attainment have been identified, together with the timing of their execution. Therefore, the TEA and TP must be defined before objectives and targets are set. Unfortunately, more often than not, objectives and targets are set with little regard for the selected strategy, the economics of the market, or the speed at which the organization can realistically transform itself. As Mankins and Steele (2005) found, failure to achieve the objectives and targets is very probable in such contexts.

Relationships Between the Concepts at the Heart of the Strategic Plan Framework

To complete our review of the Strategic Plan Framework, Figure 2.2 presents the relationships that exist between the related concepts. We have included only the main relationships of the TP and long-term financial plan with the other concepts in order not to overburden the figure. For the sake of completeness, Figure 2.2 also includes four types of business constraints – Regulations, Standards, Policies and Guidelines – that can have a significant influence on each of the

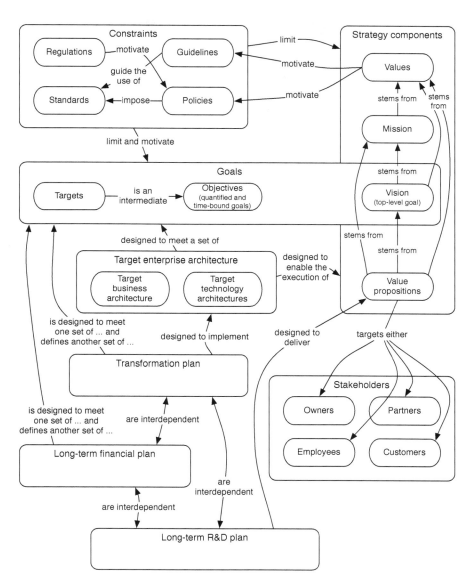

Figure 2.2: Relationships between the main concepts
at the heart of the Strategic Plan Framework

components of a strategic plan. Regulations are rules or directives made and maintained by governments or other authorities (adapted from *Oxford American Dictionary*). Standards are rules established by an authority for the measurement of quantity, weight, extent, value, or quality. They are only compulsory when imposed by regulations. Policies explain and describe standards, principles or protocols that all members of an organization must follow. Regulations and policies are hard constraints that members of the organization must abide by. Guidelines, on the other hand, are soft constraints that should be followed whenever possible.

The Number of Strategic Plans Required by Multi-Business Unit Organizations

In the case of multi-business-unit[5] organizations, one or more strategic plans may be needed, depending on several factors, the most important of which is the operating model chosen to support the organization's strategy. According to Ross et al. (2006), an operating model is the necessary level of business process standardization and integration for delivering goods and services to customers. The level of business process standardization assesses the extent to which the execution of the organization's processes will vary depending on who is performing them and where they are performed (i.e., which business unit is executing them). In turn, the level of business process integration assesses the extent to which the efforts of the various business units in the organization are linked together through shared data. Hence, using a straightforward two-dimensional model, Ross et al. (2006) contend that organizations can adopt four types of operating models depending on their process standardization and integration requirements: diversification (low standardization, low integration), coordination (low standardization, high integration), replication (high standardization, low integration), and

---

[5] By business unit, we mean an organizational unit (org unit) that has its own profit and loss statements and possibly even its own legal status.

unification (high standardization, high integration). Figure 2.3 describes the characteristics of each of the four operating models.

If we consider only the organization's operating model, the following recommendations should generally apply. Each of the daughter business units of an organization with a diversification operating model should formulate its own strategic plan, which should be financially linked to that of the parent business unit. Indeed, because each daughter business unit must compete in its own industry and must transform itself accordingly, it

	Coordination	Unification
High	**Coordination** • Shared customers, products, or suppliers • Impact on other business unit transactions • Operationally unique business units • Autonomous business management • Business unit control over business process design • Shared customer/supplier/product data • Consensus processes for designing IT infrastructure services; IT application decisions made in business units	**Unification** • Customers and suppliers may be local or global • Globally integrated business processes, often with support of enterprise systems • Business units with similar or overlapping operations • Centralized management • High-level process owners design standardized processes • Centrally mandated databases • IT decisions made centrally
Low	**Diversification** • Few, if any, shared customers or suppliers • Independent transactions • Operationally unique business units • Autonomous business management • Business unit control over business process design • Few data standards across business units • Most IT decisions made within business units	**Replication** • Few, if any, shared customers or suppliers • Independent transactions aggregated at high-level • Operationally similar business units • Autonomous business unit leaders with limited discretion over processes • Centralized (or federal) control over business process design • Standardized data definitions but data locally owned with some aggregation at corporate level • Centrally mandated IT services

Business process integration (vertical axis: High / Low)

Low   High

Business process standardization

Figure 2.3: Ross and al's (2006) four operating models

would be inappropriate for a diversified organization to impose a single strategic plan for the whole organization. Each of the daughter business units of an organization with a coordination operating model should also have its own strategic plan. However, this strategic plan should be interconnected with those of its parent and sister business units in order to capture the synergies made possible by the coordination operating model. A multi-business-unit organization with a replication operating model should have a single strategic plan that is elaborated by the parent business unit and then followed by each of the daughter business units. Finally, a multi-business-unit organization with a unification operating model should have a single strategic plan that is elaborated by the parent business unit in collaboration with its daughter business units in order to capture the strong synergies made possible by the unification operating model.

The Contribution of Business Architects to Strategy Formulation

The nature of the Formulate the Strategy group of activities can vary significantly from one organization to next. Indeed, these activities can be formal, informal, intuitive, analytical, or anything in between (Mintzberg, 1985, 1994). In addition, these activities can range from an executive-only exercise to one that encourages the generation of ideas at all organizational levels (Mintzberg, 1985, 1994; Nunes and Breene, 2011). Despite these variations, strategy formulation typically includes four main activities which together form the Formulate the Strategy process (Figure 2.4). The following paragraphs describe these four activities and the contributions business architects can make to each of them.

During the Assess Internal Environment activity, strategists identify and evaluate the organization's strengths and weaknesses, and related issues. They also gather and analyze any other internal information that can be used to formulate the strategy. Business architects should contribute to the assessment of the organization's internal environment by providing strategists with the information and insights they gathered while documenting the current business architecture (CBA) and by performing parts of the assessment themselves.

During the Assess External Environment activity, strategists identify and assess opportunities, threats and other external issues that might influence the formulation of the strategy. To do so, they must examine the current state and trends affecting the macro-environment (i.e., political, legal, economic, social, technological, ecological and climatic, and infrastructure environments) and the structure of the industry in which their organization operates (i.e., customers, competitors, suppliers, substitute products or service providers, new entrants and complementors). The necessary information can be acquired from numerous sources including customers, governments, consultants, suppliers, personal networks, external training sessions, and conferences. Business architects can contribute to the assessment of the external environment by identifying best practices adopted by competitors and key players inside and outside their organization's industry, and assessing the potential value of implementing these best practices within the organization.

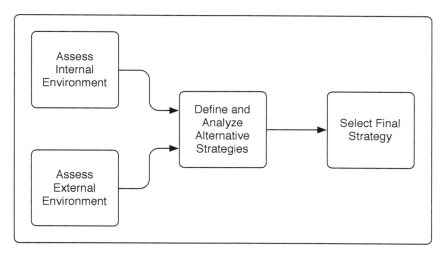

Figure 2.4: Activities of the Formulate the Strategy process
(a.k.a., Strategic Assessment-to-Selected Strategy)

The Define and Analyze Alternative Strategies activity comprises three sub-activities: Identify Alternative Strategies, Codify Alternative Strategies and Analyze Alternative Strategies. During the Identify Alternative Strategies sub-activity, strategists identify a number of alternative strategies for consideration. This sub-activity is driven by knowledge, creativity, and insight. The knowledge required during this activity stems from both the internal and external assessments, and the analysis or discovery of some patterns of events. In turn, creativity and insight may arise from anywhere in the organization. Indeed, executives and strategists are not the only people capable of generating ideas and insights; any employee may discover new opportunities from yet undetected patterns of events. Because they are exposed to a great deal of information, ideas, and insights from both inside and outside the organization, business architects are in a unique position to discover such patterns and recognize opportunities that may lead to the identification of new or improved alternative strategies.

During the Codify Alternative Strategies sub-activity, the alternative strategies are articulated in a structured manner to make them easier to understand, analyze and communicate. Although this activity should ideally be conducted by strategists, business architects may need to do it when the organization does not have such professionals.

During the Analyze Alternative Strategies sub-activity, the identified alternative strategies are analyzed based on the following three criteria: suitability, acceptability, and feasibility (Johnson et al., 2008). A suitable alternative is one that would enable the organization to achieve and maintain a competitive advantage, address the issues identified by the analysis of internal and external environments, and leverage the organization's current capabilities. Moreover, for an alternative strategy to be suitable, the organization must be able to implement it before its competitors can implement similar strategies. Acceptability refers to whether or not the benefits, risks and other impacts of a proposed alternative strategy are acceptable to all stakeholders including owners, management, employees, customers, unions, governments and the community. Feasibility assesses whether the organization has the needed capabilities – or the financial resources to build these capabilities on time – to make a given alternative strategy work. Assessing the feasibility of an alternative strategy requires that the preliminary outlines of the corresponding long-term R&D plan, TEA, TP and long-term financial plan be prepared. Indeed, assessing the feasibility of an alternative strategy requires: (1) the identification of the key investments that will be required in the coming years in fundamental research and the development of products and services; (2) the identification of the key building block transformations required for its implementation; (3) the evaluation of the benefits, costs and risks of executing these transformations; (4) the outline of a preliminary TP for executing these transformations; and, (5) that all this information be used to outline the long-term financial plan that will determine the financial viability of the alternative strategy. Business architects should contribute to the analysis of alternative strategies by outlining the TBA and TP for each one.

It is important to note that, although formal techniques must be used, the analysis of alternative strategies must leave room for intuition. Some things, such as customer demand for innovative products, are difficult to predict accurately. For example, no analysis could have anticipated that placing advertisements in glossy magazines showing black pearls together with diamonds, rubies and emeralds would successfully position black pearls as a highly sought-after luxury product (Ariely, 2008).

Finally, during the Select Final Strategy activity, one of the alternative strategies is selected for execution, its codification is perfected and the outlines of the long-term R&D plan, TEA, TP and long-term financial plan are also codified. This codification will be used later to architect the TEA, elaborate the TP, finalize the long-term R&D and financial plans and set objectives, thus completing the development of the strategic plan. Business architects should contribute to this activity by codifying the outline TBA and TP; they may also help refine and clarify the codification of the strategy.

In some situations, business architects may need to get more deeply involved in codifying the final strategy. For instance, when an organization decides to launch a business architecture practice, the first thing the business architects must do is to understand the strategy so they can architect the corresponding TBA. However, understanding the strategy may be a difficult task, because a suitable codification may not exist and there may not be anybody within the organization other than the business architects who can codify the strategy. In this situation, business architects may have to inquire what the strategy is, codify it and then validate this codification with senior executives. Through this step, executives often become aware of the important contribution made by business architects, which increases the likelihood that these professionals will be involved in the next strategy formulation cycle, as they should be. Furthermore, given that it is always preferable to define a functional area's strategy prior to architecting its TBA, business architects may be called upon to help derive these local strategies from the organization's overall strategy. In some circumstances, business architects may also be responsible for managing this process.

It is important to mention that the activities of the Formulate the Strategy process cannot be forced to conform to a specific timetable. Indeed, new ideas are bound to emerge, new information and knowledge is produced continuously, and unforeseen events, such as competitor actions and new technologies, may occur at any time. Organizations cannot wait until the end of a four-year strategy formulation cycle to react to these issues. Hence, the four strategy formulation activities should be conducted continuously, although at different levels of effort, to handle emerging strategic issues in a timely fashion. This, in turn, requires that business architects continuously support the analysis of new or improved alternative strategies.

Furthermore, it is recommended that employees working at all levels of the organization be invited to contribute to the formulation of the strategy. As Khadem (2008, p. 30) writes: "*Our advice to executives is to take as much time as necessary to involve people in formulating vision, values, and strategy.*" Indeed, as mentioned above, the generation of bright new ideas and insights is not limited to the executive suite. Employees working at all levels of the organization can uncover information and issues not visible from other vantage points, which can lead to important strategic insights. To identify these insights, we do not recommend enterprise-wide surveys or similar approaches, which generate a huge volume of data but at best collect only a few good ideas and may create employee expectations that can be hard to manage down the road. Instead, employees who excel at what they do or have a unique expertise should be interviewed to find out what they do differently and what important insights they might have. Employees who help formulate the strategy are also likely to later become ambassadors who promote its implementation and execution. Because of the work they do, business architects are in a unique position to identify potential contributors to the formulation of the strategy.

Templates Commonly used to Codify a Strategy and the Key Elements of the Corresponding Target Enterprise Architecture and Transformation Plan

This section describes six complementary templates strategists and business architects may use to codify a strategy and the key elements of the corresponding TBA, TTAs and TP. The first four templates, namely the capability-based strategy map, business model map, activity system map and SWOT matrix, codify parts of the stakeholder value propositions and the key elements of the corresponding TEA. We find these templates to be popular with executives as they condense and structure a lot of information within a small set of single-page diagrams. We remember creating one that spoke so eloquently to a COO that he carried it in his notebook for weeks. These four templates have some similarities but none of them is complete so it is rare for a single one to be sufficient to fully describe a strategy and all the key elements of the corresponding

TEA. However, it is usually not necessary to use them all. The right combination of templates depends on the type of strategy and the content of the TEA being codified. The fifth template, the capability transformation table, is used to list and provide some information about the key capabilities that must be transformed to implement a given strategy. Finally, a roadmap is used to present key transformation or R&D projects/ programs on a timeline.

The six templates should be used during strategy formulation and implementation to communicate important information to all stakeholders. During strategy formulation, they should first be used to codify each alternative strategy and the outline of the respective preliminary long-term R&D plan, TEA and TP. Then, once the final strategy is selected, its codification should be refined, using these same templates, to make it easier for all stakeholders to understand the strategy. As the full-fledged TEA and TP are being created during strategy implementation, the codification of the preliminary TEA and TP captured in these templates should be updated and augmented with other diagrams and tables.

Capability-Based Strategy Map

The capability-based strategy map is used to describe the stakeholder value propositions and identify the key building block transformations required for the organization to be able to deliver on these four value propositions (Figure 2.5). It is a variant we have developed of Kaplan and Norton's (2004) strategy map. It replaces the strategy map's financial perspective by the Owner Value Proposition Perspective and adds the Employee and Partner Value Proposition Perspectives. The capability-based strategy map embraces the concept of capabilities and of the eight types of base building blocks that make them up. Indeed, it replaces the strategy map's internal and learning and growth perspectives by the Strategic Capability Perspective and the Base Building Block Perspective, which together form a high-level description of the organization's TEA. A strategic capability is a capability that is key to delivering on one or more of

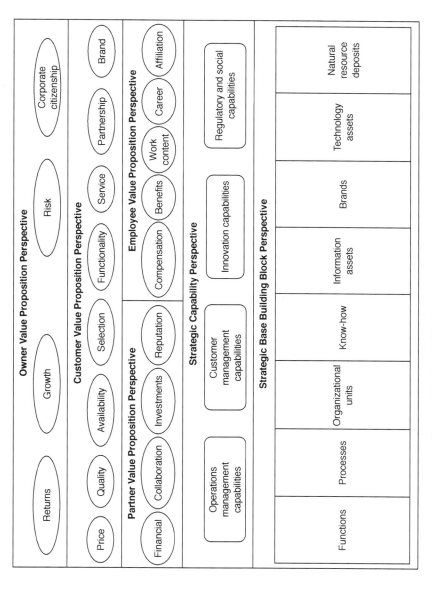

Figure 2.5: Capability-based strategy map template

the four stakeholder value propositions and that the organization has chosen as a means to differentiate itself from its competitors.

Together, the six perspectives in the capability-based strategy map present the most important attributes of the organization as it must be in the future to execute its strategy in full. Some of these attributes may already have been acquired by the organization while others may depend on the execution of some building block transformations. The latter attributes thus constitute objectives the organization has set for itself.

The six perspectives of the capability-based strategy map must be vertically linked. That is, the acquisition of the attributes in one perspective requires the acquisition of the attributes in the perspective immediately below. In other words, a base building block attribute should support the achievement of one or more capability-related attributes, which in turn should enable the organization to deliver on one or more of its target stakeholder value propositions.

Business Model Map

Osterwalder and Pigneur (2010, p. 14) define a business model as *"the rationale of how an organization creates, delivers, and captures value."* As Magretta (2002, p. 4) puts it, a business model:

> *answers Peter Drucker's age-old questions: Who is the customer? And what does the customer value? It also answers the fundamental questions every manager must ask: How do we make money in this business? What is the underlying economic logic that explains how we can deliver value to customers at an appropriate cost?*

Amongst the various possibilities available in the literature to document a business model, we prefer the one in Osterwalder and Pigneur (2010), which describes a set of position attributes tied to the customer and partner value propositions, as well as some key elements of the TEA. These authors propose a template for graphically describing a business model using nine basic components that describe exactly how a company intends to deliver value to its customers and make money while doing so (Figure 2.6 describes Skype's business model). In their book *Business Model Generation*, they define the nine basic components as follows:

- Channels (CH): *"Describes how a company communicates and reaches its Customer Segments to deliver its Value Proposition"* (p. 26).

- Customer relationships (CR): *"Describes the relationships a company establishes with specific Customer Segments"* (p. 29).

- Revenue stream (R$): *"Represents the cash a company generates from each Customer Segment (cost must be subtracted from revenues to create earnings)"* (p. 31).

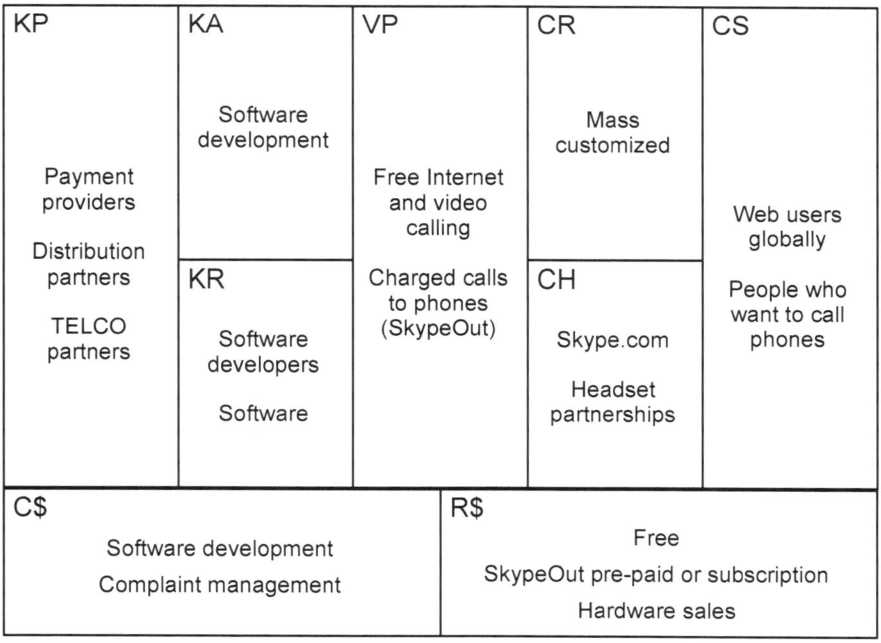

KP	KA	VP	CR	CS
Payment providers Distribution partners TELCO partners	Software development	Free Internet and video calling	Mass customized	Web users globally
	KR Software developers Software	Charged calls to phones (SkypeOut)	**CH** Skype.com Headset partnerships	People who want to call phones

C$	R$
Software development Complaint management	Free SkypeOut pre-paid or subscription Hardware sales

Figure 2.6: Map of Skype's business model
(reproduced from Osterwalder and Pigneur's (2010; p. 98))

- Key resources (KR): *"Describes the most important assets required to make a business model work"* (p. 34).

- Key activities (KA): *"Describes the most important things a company must do to make its business model work"* (p. 36).

- Key partnerships (KP): *"Describes the network of suppliers and partners that make the business model work"* (p. 38).

- Cost structure (C$): *"Describes all costs incurred to operate a business model'* (p. 40).

- Customer segments (CS): *"Defines the different groups of people or organizations an enterprise aims to reach and serve"* (p. 20).

- Value proposition (VP): *"Describes the bundle of products and services that create value for a specific Customer Segment"* (p. 22).

Activity System Map

The activity system map (Porter, 1996) identifies all the position attributes tied to the stakeholder value propositions that make up a strategy, as well as key elements of the corresponding TEA. The activity system map also shows how the position attributes and the key elements of the TEA relate and reinforce each other to form a coherent whole that is greater than the sum of its parts. Figure 2.7 is an example of an activity system map adapted from Porter (1996), which shows key elements of Southwest Airlines' customer value proposition (e.g., limited passenger service), employee value proposition (e.g., high employee compensation), and TEA (e.g., standardized fleet of Boeing 737 aircraft, which is a technology building block).

SWOT Matrix

A SWOT matrix is used to present an organization's strengths (S), weaknesses (W), opportunities (O) and threats (T) (highlighted cells in

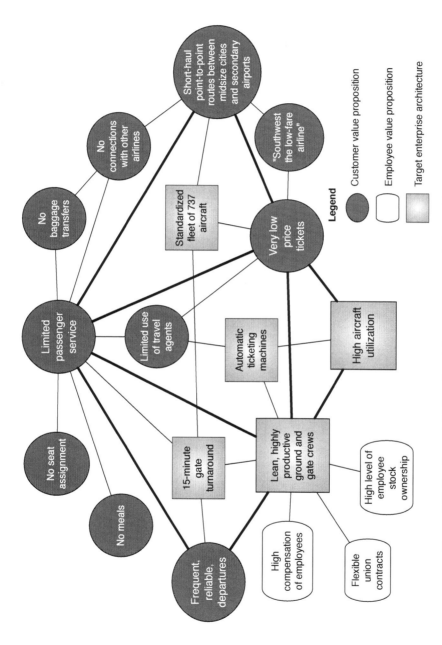

Figure 2.7: Southwest Airlines' activity system map (adapted from Porter, 1996)

Legend

Customer value proposition

Employee value proposition

Target enterprise architecture

Figure 2.8). Strengths and weaknesses are identified by assessing the organization's current capabilities while opportunities and threats are identified by assessing the external environment. The SWOT matrix is also used to identify the strategic courses of action that the organization will take to: (1) leverage its strengths to capture opportunities; (2) leverage its strengths to address threats; (3) mitigate weaknesses so opportunities can be captured; and (4) to mitigate weaknesses which may prevent the organization from reacting to threats ("course of action" cells in Figure 2.8).

Capability Transformation Table

The capability transformation table (Figure 2.9) is used to list the key capability transformations that will be required to implement a strategy and to provide some information about these transformations. This table is used to identify each capability and how it is to be transformed. There are no set rules regarding how detailed the table should be, and the level of detail does not have to be uniform throughout the table. However, we use the following three yardsticks to decide whether a transformation should be included or not in the capability transformation table: (1) the

	Strengths Strength 1 Strength 2 Strength 3	**Weaknesses** Weakness 1 Weakness 2 Weakness 3
Opportunities Opportunity 1 Opportunity 2 Opportunity 3	Courses of action related to strengths and opportunities	Courses of action related to weaknesses- and opportunities
Threats Threat 1 Threat 2 Threat 3	Courses of action related to strengths and threats	Courses of action related to weaknesses and threats

Figure 2.8: Generic SWOT template

importance of the transformation for the execution of the strategy; (2) the types and amount of resources required to execute the transformation; and (3) the amount of time that will be required to execute it.

Roadmap

A roadmap illustrates on a timeline when each of the key transformation or R&D projects/programs are planned to be executed (Figure 2.10).

Name of capability	Description of required transformation	Cost	Elapsed time to complete	Pre-requisite transformations

Figure 2.9: Capability transformation table template

	Year 1				Year 2				Year 3				Year 4			
	Q1	Q2	Q3	Q4	Q1	Q2	Q3	Q4	Q1	Q2	Q3	Q4	Q1	Q2	Q3	Q4
Project A																
Project B																
Project C																
Project D																
Project E																

Figure 2.10: Roadmap template

References

Ariely, D. (2008) *Predictably Irrational: The Hidden Forces That Shape Our Decisions*. Harper Perennial, New York.

Brandenburger, A., and Nalebuff, B.J. (1997) *Co-opetition*. Currency Doubleday, New York.

Collis, D.J., and Rukstad, M. G. (2008). Can You Say What Your Strategy Is? *Harvard Business Review*, April, 82-90.

Hax, A., Wilde, D.L., and Thurow, L. (2001) *The Delta Project: Discovering New Sources of Profitability in a Networked Economy*. Palgrave Macmillan, New York.

Johnson, G., Scholes, K., and Whittington, R. (2008) *Exploring Corporate Strategy*. Pearson Education, Harlow, UK.

Kaplan, R.S., and Norton, D.P. (2000) Having Trouble with Your Strategy? Then Map It. *Harvard Business Review*, September-October, 51-60.

Kaplan, R.S., and Norton, D.P. (2004) *Strategy Maps: Converting Intangible Assets into Tangible Outcomes*. Harvard Business Publishing, Boston.

Khadem, R. (2008) Alignment and Follow-Up: Steps to Strategy Execution. *Journal of Business Strategy*, 29(6), 29-35.

Kim, W.C., and Mauborgne, R. (2004) *Blue Ocean Strategy: How to Create Uncontested Market Space and Make Competition Irrelevant*. Harvard Business Publishing, Boston.

Magretta, J. (2002): Why Business Models Matter. *Harvard Business Review*, May, 86-92.

Maheshwari, B., Kumar, V., and Kumar, U. (2006) Optimizing Success in Supply Chain Partnerships. *Journal of Enterprise Information Management*, 19(3), 277-291.

Mankins, M.C., and Steele, R. (2005) Turning Great Strategy into Great Performance. *Harvard Business Review*, July-August, 2-10.

Minchington, B. (2010) *Employer Brand Leadership: A Global Perspective*. Collective Learning Australia, Mile End, South Australia.

Mintzberg, H. (1985) Of Strategies, Deliberate and Emergent. *Strategic Management Journal*, 6(3), 257-272.

Nunes, P., and Breene, T. (2011) *Strategy at the Edge*. Accenture Outlook, June.

Osterwalder, A., and Pigneur, Y. (2010) *Business Model Generation*. John Wiley and Sons, Hoboken, NJ.

Porter, M.E. (1980) *Competitive Strategy? Techniques for Analyzing Industries and Competitors*. The Free Press, New York.

Porter, M.E. (1996) What Is Strategy? *Harvard Business Review,* November-December, 61-78.

Ross, W.R., Weill, P., and Robertson, D.C. (2006) *Enterprise Architecture as Strategy: Creating a Foundation for Business Execution*. Harvard Business Publishing, Boston.

Sibson Consulting. (2014) *Employee Value Proposition*. [WWW document] http://www.sibson.com/services/organization-and-talent/employee-value-proposition.

Simatupang, T.M., and Sridharan, R. (2005). The Collaboration Index: A Measure for Supply Chain Collaboration. *International Journal of Physical Distribution and Logistics Management*, 35(1), 44-62.

Treacy, M., and Wiersema, F. (1995) *The Discipline of Market Leaders: Choose Your Customers, Narrow Your Focus, Dominate Your Market*. Basic Books, New York.

Chapter 3

Architecting the Target Business Architecture

Architecting their organization's target business architecture (TBA) is one of the two main responsibilities of business architects. As mentioned in Chapter 1, the TBA is a blueprint that defines how the organization must function in the future to be able to execute its strategy in full. To this end, the TBA first identifies the business capabilities, business functions, business processes, organizational units (org units), know-how assets, information assets and brands that will be needed for this purpose, and then defines the desired key features of these business architecture building blocks. Second, the TBA identifies the natural resource deposits and most important technology assets that will be needed but does not define their key features nor the functioning of the technology assets. Third, the TBA identifies and defines the desired key features of the relationships the business architecture building blocks must have with one another and with the natural resource deposit and the main technology asset building blocks. The TBA is a subset of the target enterprise architecture (TEA) which, in addition to defining how the organization must function in the future to be able to execute its strategy in full, defines how the organization's technology assets must function for this purpose.

The objective of this chapter is to describe why and how business architects should go about architecting (i.e., designing, modeling and documenting) their organization's TBA. The first section provides an overview of the TBA architecture process while the second section demystifies the core concepts that correspond to the nine types of "building blocks" used to architect the TBA. The third section clarifies a number of aspects about business architectures, models and artifacts. The fourth section describes why and how to design, document and model target business capability, business function, business process, organizational, know-how, information and brand sub-architectures. The fifth section describes how to design, model and document composite sub-architectures that include building blocks of more than one type. In addition to architecting the TBA, business architects often have to model and document three key perspectives of the target organizational context: products and services, locations, and customer segments. Thus, the sixth section describes why and how to model and document these perspectives. The seventh and last section presents the relationships between the various concepts at the heart of the TBA.

Our use of the verbs "to design," "to model," and "to document" throughout this chapter and the rest of the book must be made clear before we continue. We use these verbs as per the *New Oxford American Dictionary*, which defines "to design" as "*to decide upon the look and functioning of (something)*," "to model" as "*to devise a representation,*" and "to document" as "*to record (something) in written, photographic or other form.*" Even though each of these three verbs has a clear and distinct meaning, it must be understood that designing something necessitates the modeling of this something, and that for the model of this something to be useful, it must be documented.

To conclude this introductory section, it is important to note that the subject matter presented in this chapter is fairly complex. Indeed, the primary intent of this chapter is to provide as much information as possible for readers who aspire to become key contributors in the challenging effort of architecting their organization's TBA. Readers who seek only a high-level understanding of the TBA architecture process and related concepts can read only the first two sections of this chapter.

The TBA Architecture Process

In all but the simplest of organizations, architecting (i.e., designing, modeling and documenting) the TBA of the entire organization can require years of effort. Therefore, to sustain and succeed in such a complex and expensive endeavor, an organization needs to generate value from its TBA as it is being architected over time. This, in turn, requires that the organization adopt an approach that divides the TBA architecting effort into increments, each of which focuses on one or a few slices of the organization at a time. An incremental approach that allows the progressive design, modeling and documentation of the entire organization's TBA is best, even though new ideas and insights generated during later increments may require that previous increments be revisited. This kind of incremental approach implies that the TBA architecture process must be iterative (i.e., repeated for every new increment) and that the order in which the slices are architected must be based on their importance to the implementation of the strategy. Each iteration must also take into account changes made to the strategy, the introduction of new technologies, and other new insights gained and information learned by the organization.

The TBA architecture process must remain mostly ad hoc; it cannot be constrained by a rigid timeline or a linear set of steps. Indeed, because a TBA increment provides the most value when it generates and explores innovative ideas and new insights, and because it is difficult to know when ideas and insights will arise, the TBA architecture process must remain flexible to ensure that these ideas and insights are adequately explored and to make the most of people's creativeness. In some cases, it may even be necessary to allow the TBA architecture process to loop back.

Nevertheless, the TBA architecture process should generally comprise the following four activities: (1) initiate the project; (2) model and document the current business architecture (CBA); (3) derive the local strategies; and (4) design, model and document the TBA. During the first activity, the slice or slices of the organization to be architected are identified and a project plan is created to help manage this TBA architecting effort. Each slice of the organization to be architected can be defined in many different ways so long as the resulting slice forms a coherent whole. Selecting a number of capabilities, processes or organizational units (org units) is one of the most common ways used to define such a slice (e.g., the processes of a particular business unit or the strategic capabilities of the organization as a whole). During the second activity, the CBA of the selected slices is modeled and documented. Indeed, even though it may not have been consciously designed, every organization has a CBA that must be modeled in order to, amongst other things, facilitate the identification of building blocks that should be leveraged during the implementation of the strategy and the identification of redesign or optimization[1] opportunities that might otherwise go unnoticed. This activity should only be needed the first time the TBA of a given slice is architected because the documentation of the CBA should be updated during the ensuing projects to reflect the real building block transformations that have been made to the organization[2]. During the third activity, a local strategy for each of the selected slices is derived to determine how they can best support the whole organization's strategy. Finally, during the fourth activity, the TBA of the selected slices of the

---

[1] By redesign, we mean making an important changes in the look and functioning of something, while we use optimization to mean making minor changes to something.

[2] These transformations may be somewhat different than those planned in the TBA because of insights gained during the execution of the projects.

organization is designed, modeled and documented to improve the organization's ability to execute its strategy. During this activity, business architects should try to identify short-term wins whose rapid implementation will both show the value of the TBA as well as help break down people's natural resistance to change by demonstrating that the organization is capable of attaining its transformation objectives.

During the third and fourth activities, business architects should also define and document transformation goals for the slice, or slices, of the organization they are architecting. These goals should be derived from the stakeholder value propositions formulated in the strategy; they guide the design of the TBA and are converted into objectives and targets during the elaboration of the transformation plan (see Chapter 4).

The TBA architecture process should be managed by an individual who meets the following criteria. This person must understand the nature of the TBA architecture process and be comfortable with the fact that architecting the TBA is a winding road. This individual must also understand that, even though he/she must ensure that the TBA increments are delivered within reasonable time and cost constraints, generating and exploring innovative ideas and new insights while architecting the TBA increments is much more important for the future of the organization than delivering the increments on time and on budget. With their knowledge and background, experienced business architects are often the individuals within the organization who best meet these criteria. The role of managing the TBA architecture process may also be assigned to an experienced project manager. However, care should be taken when making such a decision since most project managers are trained to impose a linear process on the projects they undertake and thus would have a tough time managing such a non-linear process as the TBA architecture process.

The TBA architecture team should be made up of business architects and subject matter experts with knowledge relevant to the slices being architected. This team, in turn, must collaborate with executives, middle managers, IT enterprise architects and other professionals across the organization. Indeed, the TBA architecture team must gather ideas and other inputs from these stakeholders and work with them to identify and analyze design options. Without this collaboration, the TBA has little or no chance of being translated into reality because few people will understand and buy into it. In addition, this collaboration is the only way to ensure that the proposed TBA is effectively challenged.

Demystifying the Core Concepts

Business architects should use the following nine core concepts to architect their organization's TBA: business capability, business function, business process, org unit, know-how, information, technology asset, brand and natural resource deposit[3]. We recommend the use of these nine core concepts for the following two reasons. First, they allow business architects to draft models that can fully and clearly express the complexity of modern organizations. Second, they facilitate communication and collaboration between business architects and other stakeholders in the organization such as business strategists, IT enterprise architects and business process design/improvement professionals, who also rely on many of the same concepts to do their work.

The objective of this section is to demystify these core concepts, which correspond to the nine types of building blocks used by business architects to architect their organization's TBA. We have found that confusion exists about the nature of these concepts, and that they are not uniformly defined in the literature. The following paragraphs define each of the nine core concepts and explore the key differences between them. Whenever possible, we have relied on definitions provided by authoritative sources. For example, most of the business-process-related definitions come from the Object Management Group (OMG), which is a highly respected standards organization.

---

[3]   These same nine core concepts are also used to model and document the CBA.

Definitions of the Core Concepts

Business capability

The first and foremost business architecture concept is that of business capability. This concept is defined in numerous ways in the business literature. We define a business capability as "an integrated set of building blocks designed to work together to attain a specific result." This definition is based on the *New Oxford American Dictionary,* which defines a capability as *"the power or ability to do something."* It is also based on the work of several eminent authors, including Grant (1991), Makadok (2001), and Teece, Pisano and Shuen (1997), who have argued that an organization's capability to do something is the result of a team of resources (i.e., building blocks) working together.

By result, we mean a deliverable of some kind (e.g., a product manufactured, a service performed for a customer, a new employee hired, an audited financial statements, a project plan created, and a CEO-approved TBA). A result can also be a deliverable of some kind with an associated performance level that the organization already achieves or wants to achieve in the future (e.g., 2000 cars built per day, 95% of products delivered within three days after the customer order was placed). A result that specifies a performance level clarifies the nature of the associated capability. Two capabilities that produce the same deliverable but have different performance levels are distinct. The integrated set of building blocks required to produce 2000 cars a day is clearly not the same as the set required to produce a maximum of 10 cars a day.

There are two types of business capabilities: atomic capabilities and aggregate capabilities. An atomic capability is always made up of at least one of each of the following six types of building blocks: business function, business process, org unit, know-how asset, information asset, and technology asset and cannot be decomposed into lower-level capabilities. For example, to have the capability to Fabricate Metal Parts (the metal parts being the specific result), an organization must have the necessary machines (technology assets), the knowledge of how to operate them (know-how asset), the specific sequence of activities needed to fabricate the parts (process), the drawings of the parts to be fabricated (information asset), and the teams of people (org units) specializing in the various types of fabrication required to make the parts (functions). Some atomic capabilities may also require additional types of building blocks. For example, the Coca Cola Company could not sell 1.9 billion servings a day in more than 200 countries were it not for the power of its brands. In turn, for a farmer to be able to Produce Vegetables, he must have not only the first six types of building blocks but also a piece of land (natural resource deposit) on which to grow his vegetables. As shown in Figure 3.1, we refer to the eight types of building blocks that make up a atomic capability (i.e., business function, business process, org unit, know-how asset, information asset, brand, technology asset and natural resource deposit) as "base building blocks." Capabilities and base building blocks together are simply referred to as "building blocks" or "enterprise architecture building blocks." In turn, capabilities, functions, processes, org units, know-how assets, information assets and brands are also referred to as "business architecture building blocks."

As shown in Figure 3.1, an aggregate capability is made up of either two or more lower-level aggregate capabilities or two or more atomic capabilities. As an example, Figure 3.2 shows a sample of the lower-level aggregate and atomic capabilities the Formulate and Align to Strategy (FAS) aggregate capability (discussed in detail in Chapter 6) decomposes itself into. This aggregate capability is made up of two lower-level aggregate capabilities: Formulate the Strategy and Implement and Oversee the Execution of the Strategy. The Formulate the Strategy aggregate capability is made up of a set of atomic capabilities, while the Oversee the Execution of the Strategy aggregate capability is made up of lower-level aggregate capabilities which are each, in turn, made up of atomic capabilities.

Strategic capabilities are those that are key for the organization to be able to deliver on one or more of the four stakeholder value propositions and that the organization has chosen as means to differentiate itself from its competitors. They represent the bridge between the worlds of strategists and business architects. Indeed, business architects use the strategic capabilities identified by strategists during the Strategy Formulation process as the starting point for architecting the organization's TBA. Imagine, for example, that the strategists of an aerospace parts manufacturer have decided that their organization should differentiate itself from its competitors by being able to machine parts with greater

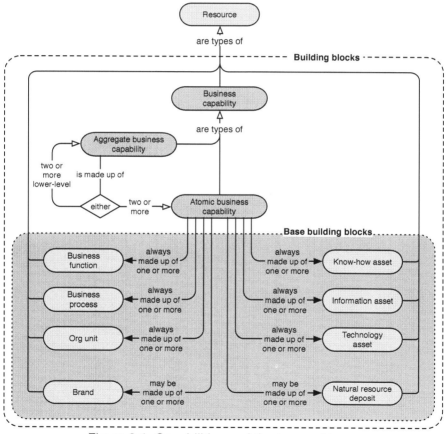

Figure 3.1: Capabilities and the types of base
building blocks they are made up of

accuracy. To achieve this differentiation, the strategists have determined that the organization must create two new capabilities: Machine Highly Accurate Metal Parts, and Develop New High-Accuracy Machining Techniques and Tools. Based on these decisions, the business architects will then architect the target architecture of these two new capabilities. This will require them to decompose each of these two capabilities into an integrated set of function(s), process(es), org unit(s), know-how asset(s), information asset(s), and technology asset(s).

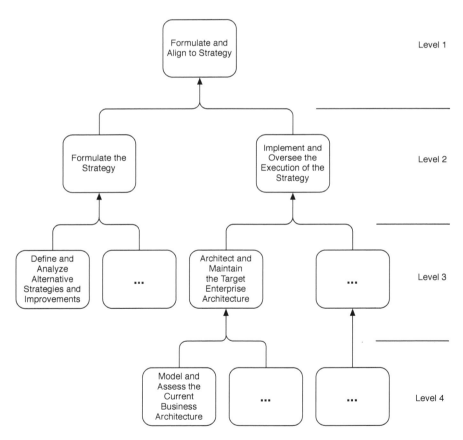

Figure 3.2: Sample of the decomposition of the
Formulate and Align to Strategy capability

Business function

A business function is a kind of work done by the organization. A business function may be made up of lower-level functions. For example, an organization's Engineering function can be made up of two lower-level functions: (1) Product Development Engineering, which relates to the design of new products; and (2) Manufacturing Engineering, which relates to the design of tools, machines, assembly jigs, and plants used to manufacture these new products. In turn, the (1) Billing, (2) Accounts Payable, (3) Accounts Receivable, and (4) Financial Reporting functions are lower-level functions of an organization's Financial Accounting function. A core function is one that provides direct value to customers (e.g., Marketing, Sales, Product Development, and Manufacturing), while support functions are those that are necessary for the organization to execute its mission but only indirectly create value for customers (e.g., Human Resource Management, Financial Resource Management, and Facility Management).

Business process

According to the OMG, a business process is *"a set of activities, methods, and practices that transforms a set of inputs into a set of products and services"* (Object Management Group, 2008, p. 463). A process can be thought of as a black box with inputs and outputs (Figure 3.3). Inside the black box is one or more activities that need to be done in a given sequence by one or more process participants in order to transform the inputs into the outputs. An activity can be a sub-process or a task. A task is a piece of work that is done by a single participant. It may

Figure 3.3: A business process viewed as a black box

involve multiple steps, in which case the sequence of steps and how they are to be accomplished are defined in a procedure. In turn, a process participant is a person or technology (e.g., machine, robot or software) that performs one or more tasks of a process. All work in an organization is done through processes. Even an ad hoc series of activities to produce a desired output is a process.

Consider for a moment the following tasks in a simple sheet metal manufacturing process: (1) cut sheet metal to the desired shape; (2) bend it to the desired profile; (3) weld it to other sheet metal parts; and (4) paint the assembly. All these tasks can be done by different people and/or machines in a modern production line. This process has a well-defined set of inputs (sheet metal and paint) and a specific output (a painted sheet metal assembly). Processes often have secondary inputs and outputs as well. In the example above, those would be respectively the specifications for the part and the recyclable scraps resulting from cutting and punching holes in the sheet metal.

Organizational unit

An organizational unit (org unit) is a team of people with a common set of goals that is headed by a manager. An organization is made up of a hierarchy of org units. The largest of these is the entire organization. An org unit that has its own profit and loss statements and possibly even its own legal standing is called a business unit. An org unit is an entity that exists on its own. It is not defined as "all of the people reporting to a given manager." Indeed, a single manager may head multiple org units. For example, in addition to leading his/her own org unit, a manager may also lead another org unit temporarily because its manager has moved on. Even though these two org units have the same manager, they are still considered separate entities.

Know-how and information assets

The next two core concepts, information and know-how, relate to the two types of knowledge held within an organization. They are not meant to replace more sophisticated knowledge classifications (Blackler, 1995; Egbu, 2004; Lam, 2000) but rather to serve the limited needs of business architects. The *New Oxford American Dictionary* defines information as *"facts provided or learned about something or someone."* Examples of such facts include, but are not limited to, the name, location and preferences of a customer; the list of items on an order; the terms of a loan; the specifications of a product; and the scope of a project. Information is explicit in nature, meaning that it can be codified in some fashion (e.g., within a document or a database) and transmitted to other people by means of this encoding.

On the other hand, know-how comprises skills and expertise. Much of an organization's know-how is held only within the brains of its members (i.e., "embrained" knowledge), either because it is difficult to codify (tacit knowledge) or because the cost of its codification is difficult to justify. Know-how with potential value for the organization is referred to as intellectual capital (IC) (McConnachie, 1997). In some circumstances, organizations may find it justifiable to codify specific know-how. This codified know-how is referred to as an intellectual asset (IA) (Sullivan, 1999). Unlike know-how that is simply classified as IC, IA does not walk out the door at the end of the workday. Finally, the organization may decide to go a step further and protect codified know-how with a patent or a copyright. An IA that is legally protected by a patent or a copyright is referred to as intellectual property, or IP (Egbu, 2004).

Business architects need to distinguish between information and know-how for two reasons. First, these two categories of knowledge are sufficiently different in nature to require the use of separate modeling techniques. Second, to function, a capability must rely on both information and know-how assets. For example, a machining capability requires both the specifications of the parts to be machined (information asset) and the skills to operate the tools (know-how asset).

Technology asset

A technology asset is a tangible or intangible asset that is the result of the application of scientific knowledge for practical purposes.[4,5] A tangible asset is "perceptible by touch" while an intangible asset is not. It is important to note, however, that a tangible asset (e.g., car) can include intangible components (e.g., software). Examples of tangible technology assets include computers, machines, cars and trucks, buildings, laboratory equipment, and telecommunication equipment, while software is an example of an intangible technology asset. Just as capabilities are the bridge between the worlds of strategists and business architects, technology assets are the bridge between the worlds of business architects and other professionals such as IT enterprise architects and manufacturing engineers who are responsible for architecting the target technology architectures (TTAs). Note that a technology asset alone does not make an organization capable of anything. It is only when it is combined with processes, know-how assets, information assets, functions and org units that the organization really becomes capable of doing something. Therefore, technology assets enable capabilities but are not capabilities in themselves.

Brand

A brand is a name and/or logo associated with a number of products and/ or services to distinguish them from other similar products and/or services, and to convey that these products and/or services share important customer value proposition attributes. For example all of Apple's laptop computers (product) are branded as MacBooks (brand)

---

4 Adapted from the New Oxford American Dictionary's definition of "technology."

5 The New Oxford American Dictionary defines science as "*The intellectual and practical activity encompassing the systematic study of the structure and behavior of the physical and natural world through observation and experimentation.*" Hence, even something as simple as a pencil can be classified a technology asset because its invention and fabrication is the result of knowledge acquired through a "*systematic study of the structure and behavior of the physical and natural world.*" That is not to say, however, that business architects should model such commonplace technology assets.

and run the Mac OS operating system (customer value proposition attribute). When a brand is registered with the Patent and Trademarks Office, it becomes a trademark. A trademark is a legal device that protects against unlawful use of the brand by anyone else, and grants the owner of the trademark exclusive rights to use the brand.

Natural resource deposit

Natural resource deposits include such things as parcels of land, natural oil and gas reservoirs, ore deposits or forests. Natural resource deposits may become exploitable as a result of the application of scientific knowledge. However, they do not come into existence as a result of such knowledge. Even though few capabilities include natural resource deposit building blocks, when they do these natural resources deposit are critical for them.

Distinctions Between the Core Concepts

To eliminate any possible ambiguity between the core concepts used to architect a TBA, the distinctions between some of these concepts must be clarified. First, a business function is not the same as an org unit. A business function represents a kind of work done by the organization while an org unit is a means of grouping people together under a manager. Although they are clearly two different concepts, the distinction between function and org unit is not always made. This confusion is probably due to the fact that organizations commonly group people into org units on the basis of the kind of work they perform. For example, people who do manufacturing work are often grouped together into an org unit called Manufacturing. A distinction should nonetheless be made between these two concepts because people can be grouped together in an org unit on many other bases than the kind of work they perform. For example, people may form an org unit because they serve the same customer market, produce similar products, or work on the same project. An org unit can also perform multiple business functions (e.g., an org unit focused on shared services may include the Human Resources, Information Technology, and Purchasing functions), while a business function may be performed by multiple org units (e.g., several business units may have their own Human Resource Management function).

Second, although the concepts of function and process are related, they need to be distinguished. To clearly distinguish between these two concepts, let us compare the functions of the lungs, heart and blood vessels to the process that takes in oxygen from the air and transports it to every cell in the body. The functions of the lungs, heart and blood vessels are respectively to transfer oxygen from the air to the red blood cells, to pump the blood, and to transport the red blood cells from the lungs to all tissues in the body and back. On the other hand, the process of taking the oxygen from the air and conveying it to every cell in a human body is as follows:

1. The lungs load red blood cells with oxygen;

2. The heart pumps blood;

3. The blood vessels channel blood throughout the body;

4. Red blood cells transfer oxygen to tissues; and

5. The heart pumps depleted red blood cells back to the lungs, and the cycle begins again.

In addition to showing the distinction between a function an a process, the example above shows the relationship that exists between these two concepts. Indeed, as Figure 3.4 shows, to deliver an output, a process requires work that belongs to different functions to be performed. Conversely, work of a given kind (i.e., work that belongs to a given function) can contribute to multiple processes.

Third, the concepts of function and know-how are closely linked but they are not the same. Indeed, although human beings require know-how to perform any kind of work, most machines perform work without having know-how. For example, the function of filling bottles can be performed by automatic bottle filling machines that cannot possess know-how.

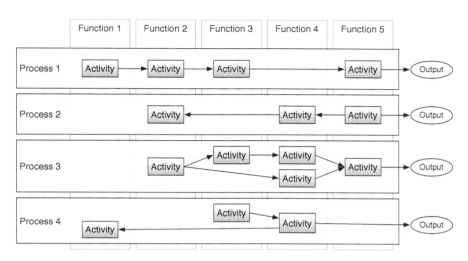

Figure 3.4: The relationship between processes and functions

Finally, contrary to the teachings of some schools of thought, business capability is not a synonym of business function or business process. To clarify the distinction between a capability, a function and a process, let us consider the example of an organization that has decided to differentiate itself from its competitors by creating and manufacturing innovative products instead of imitating other companies' products as it has done in the past. To succeed in the long run with this new strategy and maximize the likelihood of success of each of its new products, the organization will have to change the way it works. It will have to create a capability to Develop Innovative Products. This transformation will require the creation of new business architecture building blocks and/or make changes to existing ones. The organization will have to create a research function and change how existing functions such as Marketing, Engineering and Manufacturing are performed. Hence, it will have to define new processes or rework old ones. Furthermore, the organization will have to hire new employees with critical skills and motivate its entire staff to propose new product ideas. It may decide to create a new org unit and have it led by a manager with a proven track record in leading innovative teams. In addition, because the development of new products is likely to create new intellectual property, the organization will be inclined to define a process to select which intellectual capital it will want to protect with patents. As this example clearly shows, building a single business capability can be much more complex than introducing a new process or function. Indeed, in addition to requiring changes to one or more processes and functions, building a capability can also require that changes be made to other types of building blocks.

Business Architectures, Models and Artifacts

Before describing how to architect the TBA, some aspects of business architectures, models and artifacts must be clarified.

1. As shown in Figure 3.5, an organization has a CBA that defines how it currently functions. As mentioned previously, an organization's CBA exists even if it is the result of piecemeal efforts (i.e., it was not consciously designed in a holistic fashion) and is not documented. It is the result of past transformation projects executed by the organization. An organization should also have a TBA that defines how it must function in the future to be able execute its strategy in full.

2. The relationships that link together the building blocks of the CBA or the TBA can be of two types: hierarchical and peer-to-peer. There are two kinds of hierarchical relationships: decompositions and classifications. A decomposition relationship exists between two building blocks of the same type when one is a part of the other. For example, the Accounts Receivable sub-function is part of the Financial Accounting function. A classification relationship exists between two building blocks when one building block is a type of the other. For example, a car is a type of vehicle. A peer-to-peer relationship is any other type of relationship between two building blocks, whether they are of the same type or not. For example, process X relies on information system Y.

3.   As mentioned previously, the TBA should be architected by focusing
     on one or a few slices of the organization at a time. A slice can be
     defined in many ways so long as the resulting slice forms a coherent
     whole. For example, a slice can be made up of all the building blocks
     of the organization that are of a given type (e.g., all of the business
     functions), all building blocks of an org unit (e.g., all of the building
     blocks of the electronics manufacturing division) or all building blocks
     that contribute to a given capability (e.g., all building blocks of the
     Machine Highly Accurate Metal Parts capability). Each slice of the
     organization has its own sub-architecture (see Figure 3.5). A sub-

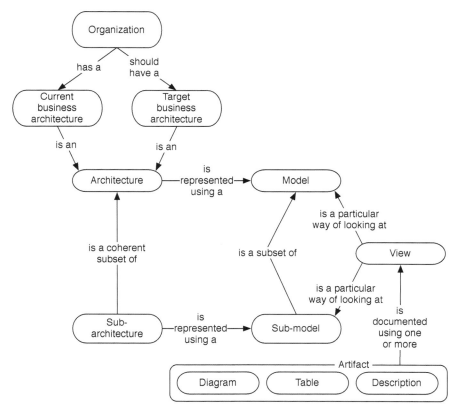

Figure 3.5: The relationships between business
architectures, models and artifacts

architecture is a subset of related building blocks that, together with the relationships that link them to one another, form a coherent whole. A sub-architecture can also describe multiple slices of the organization at once. Business architects should make sure that the target sub-architectures they architect and the current sub-architectures they model respectively coalesce into a coherent TBA and CBA of the entire organization.

4. All of the sub-architectures of the organization's CBA or TBA fall into one of several families. The first seven families, namely the business capability sub-architecture, business function sub-architecture, organizational sub-architecture, business process sub-architecture, know-how sub-architecture, information sub-architecture and brand sub-architecture families, are homogeneous as each is made up of only a particular type of building blocks. In addition to these seven homogeneous sub-architecture families, there are numerous composite sub-architecture families that are each made up of a given combination of building block types. Each of the homogeneous and composite families includes an enterprise sub-architecture that spans the entire organization (e.g., enterprise business function sub-architecture, which includes all of the functions of the organization). All of the other sub-architectures of a given family are fragments of their respective enterprise sub-architectures. Each of the homogeneous enterprise sub-architectures decomposes into multiple levels of building blocks, each of which is a type of or a part of one of the building blocks at the level directly above it.

5. As shown in Figure 3.5, a business architecture model is a representation of a given architecture. An organization's CBA and TBA can each be represented using a comprehensive model. However, because such models are usually unwieldy to work with due to their size and complexity, it is much more practical for business architects to create a series of sub-models, each of which represents a particular sub-architecture of the CBA or TBA. These

sub-models should, however, coalesce into their corresponding enterprise CBA or TBA models.

6. As depicted in Figure 3.6, models/sub-models represent an architecture/sub-architecture using both building block and relationship models. A building block model represents a building block, while a relationship model represents a relationship that links two building blocks. Each building block model or relationship model should include information about the building block or relationship it represents. We like to organize this information into groups. Each building block model and relationship model should include a general information group to capture such things as the name, type and description of the building block or the relationship it represents (Figure 3.6). A building block model may also include additional information groups. The number and types of such groups depend on

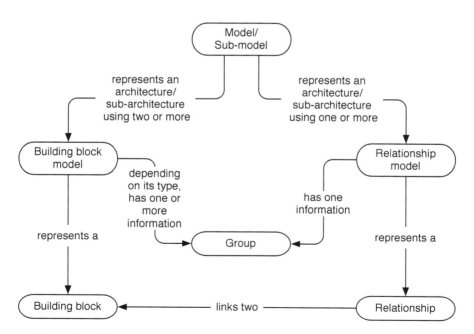

Figure 3.6: Components of a business architecture model/sub-model

the type of building block being represented. For example, the building block model of a capability, process, org unit, technology asset or natural resource deposit should have a key performance indicator (KPI) information group.[6] Additional information groups that are specific to org unit building blocks will be described in the following section.

7.   In addition to building blocks and the relationships that exist between them, models/sub-models may also include other components (e.g., stakeholder value propositions, goals, constraints, customer segments, products and services, and locations), as well as the relationships these components have with the building blocks included in the model. We will show a few examples of this later in this chapter when we present the hierarchy of process models we use in our practice.

8.   As Figure 3.5 shows, a model/sub-model can be viewed in a multitude of ways. A view is a particular way of considering or regarding a model/sub-model (adapted from the *New Oxford American Dictionary*). It always includes all of the building blocks in the model/sub-model being "looked at." A view always shows some information about each building block included in the model. A view may also show relationships that exist between the building blocks included in the model and information about these relationships. A view can be of three types: diagram, table or textual description. Based on the *New Oxford American Dictionary,* we use the word "diagram" to mean "*a schematic representation showing the appearance, structure, or workings of something,*" the word "table" to mean "*a set of facts or figures systematically displayed, especially in columns,*" and the words "textual description" to mean

---

[6] KPIs are not discussed in this book because they depend on the nature of each building block.

"written representation or account of a person, object, or event."[7] A catalog is a special type of table that contains a list of items with their descriptions and possibly other information about them.

9. One or more views of a model/sub-model can be recorded in physical (e.g., paper) and/or digital (e.g., database and electronic file) artifacts. By artifact, we mean *"an object made by a human being"* (*New Oxford American Dictionary*).

Two things that relate to business architects' specific responsibilities with respect to architecting the TBA are important to mention. First, business architects are responsible for architecting the capability, function, process, organizational, know-how and information sub-architectures but not the brand sub-architectures. The design of brand sub-architectures should remain the purview of marketing professionals. However, business architects should be involved in the process because the design of the brand sub-architectures can have far-reaching impacts on the design of the TBA's other sub-architectures. Second, although the composite sub-architectures designed by business architects should identify the most important technology assets and describe the key features of the relationships that these building blocks have with the organization's capabilities, functions, processes, org units, know-how assets, information assets and brands, business architects are not responsible for the design of the technology sub-architectures per se. Technology sub-architectures are the responsibility of other professionals within the organization. For example, IT enterprise architects are responsible for architecting the target IT enterprise architecture (TITEA) and engineers are responsible for architecting the target manufacturing technology architecture. Nevertheless, business architects should support the design of these target sub-architectures.

---

[7] Tables and textual descriptions are only discussed in this book when necessary because the types of tables and textual descriptions that must be used when modeling a TBA vary with the message to be conveyed.

Finally, we recommend the use of the following three quality criteria when modeling an organization's CBA and TBA.

- Distinct building blocks: There must not be any overlap between the definitions of the building blocks of the CBA or the TBA. The only time the content of two building blocks can overlap is when one is a part of or a type of the other (e.g., the Accounts Receivable Management function is a subset of the Financial Accounting function).

- Understandability: For maximum usefulness, a sub-model must be easy to understand by members of the organization. As such, a sub-model must use the language of the business. To achieve this, it is imperative that business architects build the business architecture sub-models in collaboration with representatives from the relevant functional areas and use business terms to name the building blocks that comprise the sub-models.

- Requisite complexity: Each sub-model should have the complexity required to adequately describe the sub-architecture of the organization it represents. Building blocks should be decomposed to the necessary level and no artificial level should be added. Some business architects build their enterprise sub-models in such a way that the base building blocks are always at the third level. We disagree with this practice because the world is not that conveniently organized. As a matter of fact, we routinely see enterprise sub-models in which some building blocks need to be decomposed only to the second level, while others require four levels or more. Other architects impose an artificial preset maximum number of building blocks per sub-model. The number 7 often comes up. Although the intention of the "maximum 7" rule is to make sub-models easier to understand, in actual fact it results in sub-models that are confusing and provide little value to the business architecture effort because they do not truly represent the organization's architecture. Overall, we find that it is better to build sub-models that decompose building blocks into as many lower-level building blocks as are required to be true to reality – no more and no fewer.

Why and How to Design, Model and Document the Seven Homogeneous Target Sub-Architectures

This section describes why and how to design, model and document a target sub-architecture of each of the seven homogeneous families: business capability, business function, business process, organizational, know-how, information and brand sub-architectures.

To lighten the text for the remainder of this book, we will minimize our use of the word "target" and use the words "architecture" and "model" to mean "sub-architecture" and "sub-model" respectively.

Business Capability Architecture

This section describes the key characteristics of a business capability architecture (BCA) and identifies the reasons why a BCA should be architected. It also present guidelines for designing a BCA and for modeling and documenting its corresponding business capability model (BCM).

Key Characteristics of a Business Capability Architecture

The key things to know about a BCA:

- As implied by its name, a BCA is made up of business capabilities and the relationships they have to one another.

- A BCA includes hierarchical relationships of the decomposition type. That is, a BCA decomposes high-level capabilities into lower- and lower-level capabilities. In addition, because a capability often needs the support of capabilities other than its own lower-level ones, a BCA also includes peer-to-peer relationships.

Why Design, Model and Document a Business Capability Architecture?

The reasons why a BCA should be architected are:

- To bridge the gap between an organization's strategy and the design of its building blocks. While the strategy identifies how the organization wants to behave in the future, the objective of a target BCA is to identify and describe, using the language of the business, the set of capabilities that will be needed to execute this strategy.

- To help design an organizational architecture that will propel the transformation of the organization. Indeed, having a BCA enables the design of an organizational architecture that clearly identifies who will lead, or otherwise contribute to, the transformation of each of the organization's capabilities and gives them decision rights commensurate with their responsibilities.

- To help IT enterprise architects design the corresponding TITEA. The job of IT enterprise architects is to do exactly this in collaboration with business architects. Consequently, IT enterprise architects must have a detailed understanding of the corresponding target BCA.

- To facilitate the work of business continuity and IT disaster recovery professionals. By determining the criticality of each capability, these professionals can infer the criticality of their constituent building blocks.

Guidelines for Designing a Business Capability Architecture

First, the strategy (i.e., values, mission, vision, and stakeholder value propositions) and the long-term R&D plan are prerequisites for designing a target BCA.

Designing the enterprise BCA starts with the mission. In addition to identifying the organization's purpose, the mission also represents the highest-level description of what the organization must be capable of doing. Thus, the mission is the capability at the topmost level of the enterprise BCA. The mission is then decomposed into lower- and lower-level capabilities until every capability has been subdivided enough to adequately describe what the organization must be able to do to execute its strategy.

The codification of the strategy is the first place to look when seeking to identify strategic capabilities. Interviews with business leaders can also help to identify and validate these strategic capabilities and reveal non-strategic capabilities. A good way to proceed is to start with the organization's executives to identify the capabilities they own, and then move downward through the organizational structure.

Guidelines for Modeling and Documenting a Business Capability Model

We use a simple fill-in-the-blank technique to determine the name of each business capability. This technique requires the completion of the following sentence: "To execute our strategy, we must be able to _____." The two examples of strategic business capabilities mentioned in the "Definitions of the Core Concepts" section, namely Machine Highly Accurate Metal Parts and Develop New High-Accuracy Machining Techniques and Tools, are examples of properly identified and named business capabilities.

Some of the general information that should be captured about each capability included in a BCM is shown in Table 3.1.

In our practice, we like to rely on three types of views to document a BCM: business capability city maps, network diagrams, and tables. A business capability city map diagram represents a decomposition of the organization's capabilities (Figure 3.7). This type of diagram is called a "city map" because it is similar to a map of a city which shows its boroughs, which in turn are made up of city blocks, which, in turn, are made up of buildings. This kind of diagram is well suited to show a wide array of business capabilities. A business capability network diagram describes the hierarchical and peer-to-peer relationships between the capabilities of the organization. Figure 3.8 shows a generic example of a business capability network diagram. We usually create all or part of the enterprise capability city map diagram, a series of capability network diagrams, each representing one or more slices of the organization, and various tables.

Table 3.1: Some of the general information to be captured
about each capability included in a BCM

Information	Description
Name	Name of the capability
Strategic	Is the capability strategic or not?
Type	Type of capability (Core or Support)*
Alignment with strategy	Extent to which the capability is aligned with the strategy (High, Medium, Low or No)
Business continuity criticality	Business continuity criticality level of the capability (Critical, Very High, High, Medium or Low)
Life cycle phase	Life cycle phase the capability is in (Planned/In development/In production)
Transformation priority	Transformation priority assigned to the capability (Critical, Very High, High, Medium or Low)
Regulatory compliance	Regulatory compliance level of the capability (Partial or Complete)
Current functioning	Description of how the capability currently functions
Target functioning	Description of how the capability should function in the future

* A core capability is one that provides direct value to customers, while a support capability creates value for the customer indirectly.

Business Function Architecture

This section describes the key characteristics of a business function architecture (BFA) and identifies the reasons why a BFA should be architected. It also present guidelines for designing a BFA and for modeling and documenting its corresponding business function model (BFM).

Key Characteristics of a Business Function Architecture

The key things to know about a BFA:

- As implied by its name, a BFA is made up of business functions and the relationships they have to one another.

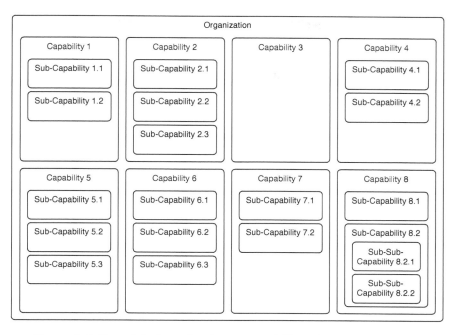

Figure 3.7: Template for a business capability "city map" diagram

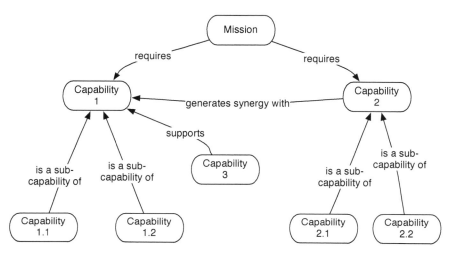

Figure 3.8: Generic example of a business capability network diagram

- A BFA includes only hierarchical relationships of the decomposition type. Indeed, a BFA decomposes high-level functions into lower- and lower-level functions.

- A BFA includes functional roles. A functional role identifies the kind of work done by a process participant. A functional role is made up of the group of lower-level functions that a given participant is called upon to perform in one or more processes. Multiple functional roles may be assigned to the same person. For example, a store manager may manage the store but may also play the functional role of head cashier and, occasionally, of cashier as well.

Why Design, Model and Document a Business Function Architecture?

The reasons why a BFA should be architected are:

- To facilitate the design of the organizational architecture. Even though several dimensions (e.g., product, geography and market) can be used to draw the lines that separate org units, the functional dimension is the most common. When designing an organizational architecture of a slice of the organization, understanding the BFA of this slice is therefore a prerequisite.

- To facilitate the work of process designers. A functional role catalog enables process designers to reuse previously defined functional roles, when appropriate, instead of inventing new ones every time a new process is designed. This catalog is also very useful when configuring information system security.

Guidelines for Designing a Business Function Architecture

The prerequisites for designing the BFA of a slice of the organization are:

- The strategy;

- The constraints (i.e., regulations, guidelines, policies and standards); and

- The corresponding BCM.

Designing a BFA starts with the identification of the top-level functions, which are then subdivided into lower- and lower-level functions and so on until the level of atomic functions is reached. By atomic function, we mean a function that cannot be decomposed any further.

Guidelines for Modeling and Documenting a Business Function Model

To name a business function, we use either a noun (e.g., marketing, finance, engineering) or a compound noun such as "project management" or "financial forecasting."

A BFM should classify kinds of work solely on the basis of their nature and not on where they are performed in the organization. Therefore, business architects should resist pressures from other stakeholders who would like to reproduce the organizational structure in a BFM for fear that doing otherwise may lead to organizational structure changes and a loss of responsibilities for them.

Because devising a BFM from scratch can be a complex task, public frameworks should be used to accelerate the process. There are a number of public frameworks available today that classify some of the work done by organizations. Some of them are generic while others focus on specific industries or functions. Caution is nonetheless required when using such frameworks. Indeed, a BFM should be adjusted when necessary to suit the nature of an organization. As demonstrated by the fact that updates to public frameworks are regularly published, work classification is not an exact science. In addition, it is very important that the members of the organization perceive the enterprise BFM as being well devised and truly reflecting the nature of the work done within the organization. When no public framework is sufficiently representative of the organization's nature, a framework should still be used as a starting point to identify the common business functions (e.g., finance, HR, IT). The names of the functions in public frameworks can be changed to reflect the terms and naming convention used within the organization. However, the names of the functions in the public framework should also be kept as references to facilitate access to performance benchmarks published by the organizations that created the public framework used.

The American Productivity and Quality Center's (APQC's) Process Classification Framework[SM] (PCF) is an example of a public classification framework that can be used to devise a BFM. The APQC PCF classifies processes according to their purpose (i.e., the main function they serve). Most of the APQC process categories (Figure 3.9) and groups (Figure 3.10) are level 1 and level 2 functions. Hence, the APQC's PCF is similar to a tree whose branches are functions and whose leaves are processes. In addition to the APQC, which covers the largest number of industries, several other bodies such as ACORD, the Telemanagement Forum, ITIL, the Supply Chain Council, and the Value Chain Group also offer either industry-specific or business-function-specific classifications. The scope

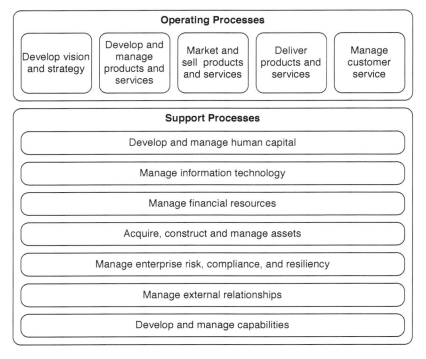

Figure 3.9: APQC process categories

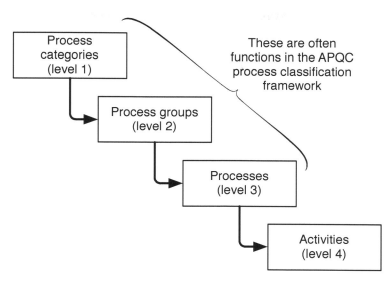

Figure 3.10: APQC PCF structure

covered by each of these bodies is shown in Table 3.2. In cases where appropriate industry-specific and business-function-specific classifications are not available, the APQC's generic PCF, which includes functions common to nearly all industry types, can be used as a starting point and adapted to the specifics of the organization's industry.

Some of the general information that should be captured about each function included in a BFM is shown in Table 3.3.

In our practice, we like to rely on two types of views to document a BFM: city map diagrams and tables. A business function city map diagram shows the decomposition of high-level functions into lower- and lower-level functions. Figure 3.11 is an example of a city map diagram that shows some of the functions performed by a city hall. We also like to create a functional role catalog, which is a simple table comprising the name and description of each functional role together with the lower-level functions they perform.

Table 3.2: Scope of the process classifications
published by various bodies

Industry	ACORD	APQC	ITIL	Supply Chain Council	TM Forum	Value Chain Group
Generic		X				X
Banking		X				
Aerospace and defense		X				
Automotive		X				
Broadcasting		X				
Consumer products		X				
Education		X				
Electric utilities		X				
Insurance	X					
IT operations			X			
Petroleum downstream		X				
Petroleum upstream		X				
Pharmaceutical		X				
Retail		X				
Supply chain				X		
Telecom		X			X	

Table 3.3: Some of the general information to be captured
about each business function in a BFM

Information	Description
Name	Name of the function
Description	The type of work that comprises this function
Type	Type of function (Core or Support)
Centralization of the function	Is the function centralized or decentralized?
Outsourced	Is the function outsourced or not?
Regulatory compliance	Regulatory compliance level of the function

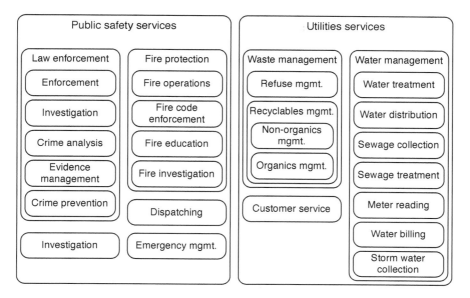

Figure 3.11: Example of city map diagram that shows some of the functions performed by a city (levels 1, 2 and 3)

Business Process Architecture

This section describes the key characteristics of a business process architecture (BPA) and identifies the reasons why a BPA should be architected. It also presents guidelines for designing a BPA and for modeling and documenting its corresponding business process model (BPM).

Key Characteristics of a Business Process Architecture

The key things to know about a BPA:

• As implied by its name, a BPA is made up of business processes and the relationships they have to one another.

• A BPA includes two types of processes: processes that are made up of tasks and macro-processes that are made up of lower-level processes. Macro-processes are also known as end-to-end processes.

- A BPA includes hierarchical relationships of the decomposition type. Indeed, a BPA decomposes macro-processes into lower- and lower-level processes. In addition, because many of an organization's processes are linked together by the fact that the outputs of some are the inputs of others, a BPA also includes peer-to-peer relationships.

Why Design, Model and Document a Business Process Architecture?

The reasons why a BPA should be architected are:

- To enable the execution of the strategy. Strategy execution requires that the organization's processes be aligned with the strategy. Designing the BPA and redesigning the misaligned processes is the first step in making the organization's strategy operational. The second step is the implementation of these new processes.

- To facilitate employee training. The use of the BPM makes it easier to train employees in the activities they have to perform.

- To facilitate operational risk and regulatory compliance management. Having a BPM enables Governance, Risk and Compliance (GRC) professionals to review the design of individual processes in order to identify activities that should be subject to controls to mitigate operational risks and ensure compliance.

Guidelines for Designing a Business Process Architecture

The prerequisites for designing the BPA of a slice of the organization are:

- The strategy;
- The constraints;
- The Products and Services Classification (discussed later in this chapter);
- The corresponding BCM; and
- The corresponding BFM.

Any BPA design effort should start with the mapping of the current macro-processes, followed by the design of the corresponding target macro-processes. The redesign or optimization of a macro-process may require that existing processes be modified and/or removed, that new processes be added, or that the sequence of execution of the processes be modified. Focusing first on macro-processes is crucial for two reasons:

- Mapping current macro-processes is necessary to understand how the organization's current processes interact with each other. Indeed, mapping current macro-processes often exposes important flaws, including non-optimal process sequences, processes making do with inadequate inputs, and, in some cases, incompatible practices.

- Redesigning macro-processes can generate important gains. In fact, no amount of redesign or optimization at the process level will ever generate as much benefit as when the macro-processes are redesigned or optimized first. The redesign or optimization of a macro-process requires discussions between members of different org units to review the current macro-process design and resolve any issues that have been identified. Even though these discussions can be arduous, the gains can be significant. Unfortunately, people often avoid this step because of the politics associated with such discussions.

Once a macro-process has been redesigned or optimized, each of its constituent processes should be optimized, completely redesigned, or, if new, designed from scratch. Various methodologies are available to optimize existing processes. The three most popular are Lean, Six Sigma and the Theory of Constraints.

Even though the DMAIC process (i.e., Define, Measure, Analyze, Improve, Control) at the heart of Lean, Six Sigma and the Theory of Constraints is similar, the objectives of the three methodologies differ:

- Lean focuses on increasing process efficiency (i.e., reducing time, costs and/or work that adds no value);

- Six Sigma focuses on increasing process effectiveness through improved quality and reduced variability; and

- The Theory of Constraints focuses on improving the throughput of a process by identifying the bottlenecks (i.e., the constraints) and alleviating them by various means until the desired throughput is reached.

These three methodologies can be used together and, although they were developed for the manufacturing industry, they have also been used successfully in other sectors such as banking, services, software development, higher education, government, and pharmaceutical. It is important to note, however, that not all types of processes benefit from such rigorous optimization. For example, it has been found that product and service innovation can be significantly hampered by the rigidity that results from such process optimization (Nunes and Breene, 2011).

Another way to optimize a process is to analyze the operational risks inherent to its design and to modify the process in order to mitigate risks that are judged to be too large. This can be done by adding controls in the process or changing how some tasks are performed.

In some situations, process optimization will not suffice. This is often the case when:

- A process must be redesigned to align it with the organization's stakeholder value propositions.

- A process must be redesigned to align it with the target design of the macro-process to which it belongs.

- The practice underlying a process must be changed (e.g., changing an organization's budget allocation process from a yearly process to a 12-month rolling forecast updated every month).

- A new process must be designed.

In such situations, the design philosophies proposed by Lean, Six Sigma and the Theory of Constraints can still be used even though DMAIC cannot help. The use of the three design philosophies ensures that the process to be designed/redesigned is optimized right from the start. A process design/redesign should also include operational risk analysis and mitigation.

Large organizations with business functions distributed throughout multiple business units may need to design target "conceptual" processes to set minimal common requirements and ensure some degree of uniformity between the various business units' "operational" processes. A conceptual process, also called a "functional process," identifies the minimal activities and the business functions that must perform them. It is non-executable and hence must be translated into an "operational" process designed for the particular context of each business unit before it can be executed. Each business unit must translate the activities of the target conceptual process into more specific tasks and identify which functional roles will perform each task.

Guidelines for Modeling and Documenting a Business Process Model

Business processes should be given a technical name that uses an "A-to-B" format, where "A" and "B" are usually the names of the activities or events that start and end the process. This naming convention is also recommended by Hammer and Champy (2006). For example, the "Lead-to-Order" process starts when a sales lead (start event) has been identified and ends once the customer has placed an order (end event). Similarly, the "Order-to-Cash" process starts once the customer places an order (start activity) and ends once the customer's payment is received (end event). Other examples of technical process names include Position opening-to-Hire, Concept-to-Product, and Procure-to-Pay. This naming convention, the purpose of which is similar to that of biologists' use of Latin and Greek to create "scientific" names for animal and plant species, is very useful in distinguishing processes from functions. Indeed, whenever it is difficult to identify the start and end activities/events of a group of related activities, it is probably because those activities do not in fact form a process. In such a situation, it is more likely that the activities identified are related because they are part of the same function.

Although the use of technical names is common and well accepted in some industries, others may find this naming convention difficult to work with. When that is the case, processes can also be given a common name using a "verb object" format, such as "Allocate budget" or "Design target architecture." The use of the verb "manage" should, however, be avoided because it is too vague. We must emphasize here that the common names of processes are often very similar to those of related capabilities, which can lead to confusion. That is why we personally prefer to refer to processes by their technical names.

Some of the general information that should be captured about each business process included in a BPM is shown in Table 3.4.

Because a BPM is very complex, it must be broken down into a hierarchy of models that describe how the organization's processes should interact with one another and how each process should work. Figure 3.12 shows the hierarchy of process models we use in our practice. It is based on the work of Harmon (2003), Barros (2007), and Hammer and Champy (2006) and our own experience modeling business processes. The hierarchy starts at the top with the organizational environment model, which represents the organization as it appears from the outside: a "black box" with multiple inputs and outputs. This model also shows with which stakeholder groups the organization exchanges these inputs and outputs. The organizational context model is documented using a diagram such as the one shown in Figure 3.13. All major input and output groups should be shown on this diagram. Secondary inputs and outputs should only be shown in diagrams that document lower-level processes.

Once the organizational environment model has been created, the high-level macro-process model can be built. This model identifies the organization's macro-processes and how they are related to one another

Table 3.4: Some general information to be captured
on each business process in the BPM

Information	Description
Name	Name of the process
Type	Is it a macro-process or a process?
Parent capability	Name of parent capability
Documented	Is the process documented or not?
Alignment with the strategy	Extent to which the process is aligned with the strategy (High, Medium, Low or No)
Regulatory compliance	Regulatory compliance level of the process (Partial or Complete)
Inherent operational risk level	Operational risk level of the process before mitigation (Critical, High, Moderate, Low, Very Low)
Residual operational risk level	Operational risk level of the process after mitigation (Critical, High, Moderate, Low, Very Low)
Transformation priority	The level of priority assigned to the transformation of this process (High, Medium or low)
Current functioning	Description of how the process currently functions
Target functioning	Description of how the process should function in the future

and to the major input and output groups included in the organizational context model. Hire-to-retire is an example of a macro-process. It starts with the opening of a position and ends once the employee hired to fill that position leaves the organization (e.g., retiring, moving on to new opportunities, being fired). By position we mean the place occupied by a person in the organization's vertical organizational structure (discussed later in this chapter). This macro-process also includes processes related to such things as performance appraisals, promotions and training. A high-level macro-process model is documented using a diagram such as the one shown in Figure 3.14.

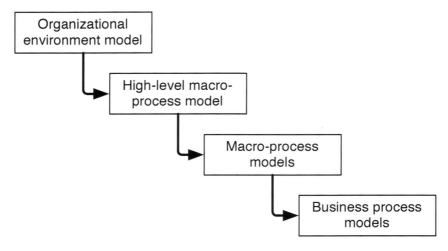

Figure 3.12: Hierarchy of process models

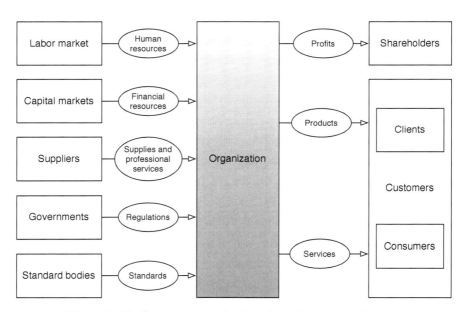

Figure 3.13: Generic organizational environment diagram

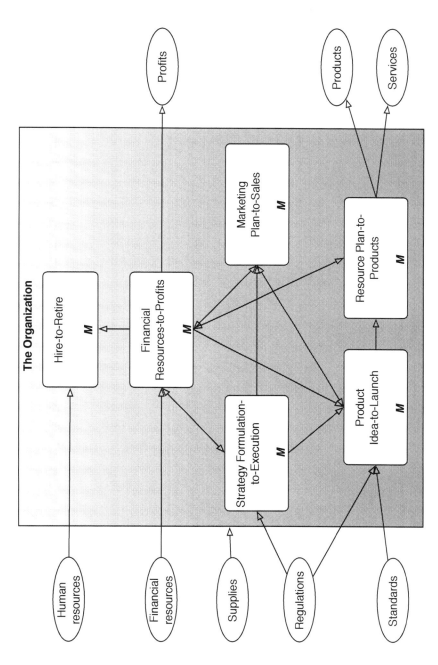

Figure 3.14: Example of a high-level macro-process diagram

Next, a model for each macro-process can be created. A macro-process model identifies the processes that make up the macro-process and the information and material flows between each of them. A macro-process model is documented using a diagram such as that shown in Figure 3.15. This type of diagram is very useful when optimizing a process for quality, amongst other things. Indeed, it is common for the outputs of a process to lack quality, not because of the design of the process itself but because of the inadequate quality of the inputs it uses. If a diagram of the macro-process is available, the processes that provide these inputs can be readily identified.

A macro-process diagram generally does not identify process participants. The only exception to this rule is when a macro-process includes processes that are carried out completely by business partners or government bodies and that are unlikely to be replaced by internal processes. Since such external processes constrain the optimization of the macro-processes they belong to, to some degree, it can be useful to show in the macro-process diagram that they are indeed external to the organization, as depicted in Figure 3.15.

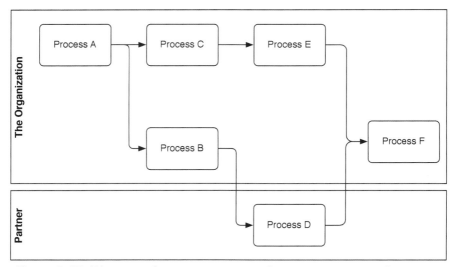

Figure 3.15: Diagram of a macro-process that uses an external process

The hierarchy of models ends with process models. A process model describes an individual process and is documented using a process diagram such as a swimlane, SIPOC (which stands for Supplier, Input, Process, Output, and Customer) or value stream diagram. Each of these types of process diagrams offers a different view. Hence, the type of process diagram used will depend on the type of process analysis being done and on what is to be communicated. A swimlane diagram is the most appropriate type of process diagram to describe in detail the flow of tasks that make up a process. SIPOCs, on the other hand, are more appropriate for Six Sigma analyses, while value streams are more suited for Lean analyses. Because they are the most commonly used, we will only discuss swimlane diagrams here.

A swimlane process diagram graphically describes the flow of activities (i.e., sub-processes and tasks) within a process and identifies the participants that perform each activity. This type of process diagram got its name from the fact that it looks like an Olympic swimming pool viewed from above. Indeed, it is subdivided into a series of parallel rectangles, or lanes, that are used to show the tasks performed by different process participants. These lanes should be associated with functional roles or business functions, not org units, positions or people. The reason for this is that functional roles are relatively stable over time whereas org units, positions and people change frequently. If org units, positions or people were used, swimlane process diagrams would need to be updated every time a reorganization occurred or a new person was assigned to a functional role. An example of a swimlane process diagram built using the BPMN[8] notation is shown in Figure 3.16.

A swimlane process diagram also documents the inputs and outputs of the process together with the events that start the process and the ones the process generates. In addition, it may show the information created

---

[8] BPMN, which stands for business process model and notation, is a standard that was initially developed by the Business Process Management Initiative (BPMI) and is now maintained by the Object Management Group.

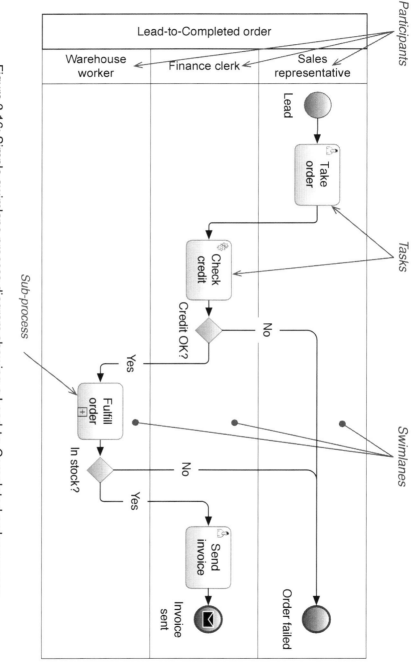

Figure 3.16: Simple swimlane process diagram showing a Lead-to-Completed order process (adapted from Silver, 2011)

and used. It may also show the information systems used, as well as the (inherent and residual) operational risks associated with its activities and the controls added to mitigate them. The leading process modeling software packages available on the market are able to turn the display of this extra information on or off. Some business process modeling software packages also provide a simulation functionality that facilitates process performance assessment. To use this simulation functionality, the process model must be supplemented with information such as the average time it takes to execute each activity, and the average wait time between consecutive activities.

In addition to the diagrams described above, it may sometimes be necessary to create simplified macro-process diagrams or process diagrams to facilitate some types of communication (e.g., an executive presentation or discussions at the initial stage of designing a macro-process or process). Simplified macro-process/process diagrams can be created to show only the key processes/activities.

Organizational Architecture

This section introduces the complex topic of organizational architecture. It describes the key characteristics of an organizational architecture (OA) and identifies the reasons why an OA should be architected. It also presents guidelines for designing an OA and for modeling and documenting an organizational model (OM). For more information on this topic, we refer the reader to the works of Galbraith (2002), Kates and Galbraith (2007), Rogers and Blenko (2006), Blenko, Mankins and Rogers (2010), Blenko and Davis-Peccoud (2011) and Mintzberg (1979).

Key Characteristics of an Organizational Architecture

The key things to know about an OA:

- An OA includes an organizational structure (OS), which defines how the organization's workforce is subdivided into teams (i.e., org units), each of which is headed by a manager and has its own mission. The most visible part of the OS in most organizations is the organizational chart.

- An OS is made up of a hierarchical (or vertical) sub-structure, which decomposes the entire organization into lower- and lower-level org units until the level of individual positions is reached. We call the teams that result from this hierarchical decomposition vertical org units. Every vertical org unit has one or more positions associated with it which are each occupied by a member of the organization. Typically, one of these positions is that of manager. In addition, an OS also includes non-hierarchical (or horizontal) sub-structures such as multidisciplinary project teams and committees. These non-hierarchical sub-structures are called horizontal org units. A horizontal org unit is a permanent or temporary team that brings together people from one or more vertical org units to facilitate the coordination and decision-making required to achieve particular goals. Hence, an OS includes both hierarchical relationships of the decomposition type and peer-to-peer relationships.

- An OA also identifies the decision rights associated with each of the important decision types made within the organization. By decision type, we mean a group of decisions that are similar in nature or that pertain to the same subject (e.g., strategy decisions, product design decisions, production planning decisions, customer discount decisions, TBA decisions).

- An OA also defines bonuses and other incentives used to reward the people who are accountable for achieving business objectives, as well as the rules governing the awarding of those incentives.[9]

---

[9] This characteristic only applies to organizations that rely on incentives to motivate their people.

Why Design, Model and Document an Organizational Architecture?

The reasons why an OA should be architected are:

- At the risk of stating the obvious, to organize the members of the organization into teams that can be managed effectively and efficiently.

- To define the missions of the org units the organization is made up of in such a way that they complement one another and do not overlap.

- To facilitate decision-making within the organization. By allocating decision rights for the most important decision types, an OA clarifies the roles assigned to each stakeholder involved in making decisions. Blenko, Mankins and Rogers (2010) have shown that this clarification can significantly improve the performance of organizations. They write that:

decision effectiveness and financial results correlate at a 95 percent confidence level or higher for every country, industry, and company size we studied. Top-quintile companies on decisions generate total shareholder returns nearly 6 percentage points higher than of other companies. (Blenko, Mankins and Rogers, 2010, p. 267)

Conversely, the authors found that organizations that do not explicitly allocate decision rights face some or all of the following issues (Blenko, Mankins and Rogers, 2010), which negatively impact their performance:

- Decisions/recommendations may not be made/prepared by the right stakeholders or may be delayed while stakeholders try to determine who should be responsible for making or recommending them.

- Decision-making may require more effort than necessary and lead to lower-quality decisions.

- Accountability for a decision may be difficult to determine. This makes it difficult to give credit to people who are responsible for good decisions and identify those responsible for bad ones.

- Conflicts between org units or between the organization and its partners may arise if one party makes a decision independently of its counterpart when the other party believes it should have been responsible for or involved in making the decision.

Guidelines for Architecting an Organizational Architecture

The following paragraphs present: (1) general guidelines to be followed when designing an OA; (2) guidelines for designing an OS; (3) guidelines for identifying the most important decision types and designing related decision rights; and (4) guidelines for modeling and documenting an OM.

Regarding the guidelines that pertain to incentives, we will limit our discussion to the following two points. First, incentives should be tied to the achievement of strategic objectives cascaded down from the top of the organization. Second, the selection of proper metrics to measure the achievement of strategic objectives is crucial since selecting the wrong ones can encourage undesirable behaviors.

General Design Guidelines

The prerequisites for designing the OA of a slice of the organization are:

- The strategy;

- The constraints;

- The corresponding BCM;

- The corresponding BFM;

- The transformation plan; and

- in some cases, the long-term R&D plan.

An organization's OA should be aligned to its strategy. Indeed, a properly designed OA defines an OS, decision rights and incentives that facilitate and encourage the implementation and execution of the strategy. It is also important for this alignment to persist over time. Hence, any time a change is made to the organization's strategy, a corresponding change to the OA may be needed. To illustrate this, let us consider a fictitious organization whose strategy is to provide services to local small businesses across the country and to tailor these services to regional preferences. This organization has aligned its OA to its strategy by (1) creating regional business units; (2) making the leader of each regional business unit accountable for his/her unit's financial results; and (3) allowing each business unit to create its own local sales, market research and service design teams. This alignment has enabled the organization to significantly increase its market share over the last decade. If this organization were to change its strategy to continue its growth by providing services to larger nationwide businesses that demand identical services across all of their locations, the organization would have to make a corresponding change to its OA. It would need to centralize its sales, market research and service design teams, and transform its regional business units to enable them to focus on the delivery of the standardized services demanded by the new customers. In addition, changes would need to be made to the objectives and incentives assigned to the leaders of the regional business units to motivate them to support the standardization effort.

Instead of being designed based on political maneuverings, an OA should be the result of rigorous analyses and the weighing of the pros and cons of various alternatives.

The design of an OA is always an exercise in compromise as no organizational architecture is ever perfect. However, there is always an OA that represents the best fit with a particular strategy.

Before changing its OA, an organization must make sure the OA is actually the root cause of the problems it is facing. Organizations are often very quick to assume that the problems they are facing originate from their OA, and since these problems often have their real origins elsewhere in the organization (e.g., processes), the organizational changes they make in an attempt to resolve these problems often do not deliver the desired benefits and can even damage their OA. What is worse, by creating the illusion that the problems have been fixed, these changes allow the problems to linger on and possibly become even more acute before their real root causes are identified and properly rectified.

Once a new OA is implemented, it must be given enough time to succeed. The more drastic the change, the more time is required for the organization to assimilate the new organizational architecture. Indeed, when an OA is changed, managers need time to assess the performance of the business functions they have inherited and transform them as necessary. They also need time to assess whether these building block transformations have delivered on their objectives and determine if further transformations are needed. In addition, the staff must be given time to adjust to the changes. The same is true when the allocation of decision rights is changed. Time is needed to determine whether or not the changes have had the desired effects.

Organizational Structure Design Guidelines

An OS should be designed using a top-down approach. The first step is to identify the slices of the organization whose structure is to be designed. The second step is to divide these slices into a number of vertical org units and complement them with horizontal org units. The third step is to determine if and how the resulting vertical and horizontal org units should be further subdivided into lower-level org units. This last step is repeated until there are no more org units that must be further subdivided.

According to Kates and Galbraith (2007), an org unit can be vertically divided along the following dimensions: business function, product line, customer segment, geographic segment, project or process. Most of the time, a single dimension is used. Examples of divisions along each of the six dimensions are presented below:

- Business function: The top level of a product manufacturing organization is divided into functional areas such as marketing, engineering, manufacturing, human resources, and finance.

- Product line: A high-voltage electric components manufacturer is divided into control products, measurement products, and motors and generators org units.

- Customer segment: A bank has one org unit responsible for personal banking and another responsible for corporate banking.

- Geographic segment: An international consulting company is divided into several business units, each responsible for delivering services in a specific geographic area.

- Project: An engineering firm working on large multi-year projects creates an org unit for each major new project and moves engineers in and out of these org units as needed. Contrary to horizontal project org units, the members of these vertical project org units do not belong to any other org unit.

- Process: A manufacturing department is divided into a number of subunits that are each responsible for the execution of a particular process that encompasses all of the parts manufacturing, assembly, quality control and packaging activities related to a single product.

It is important to mention here that more than one business function, product line, customer segment, geographic segment, project or process may be assigned to each of the resulting subunits. For example, when one divides an org unit along the business function dimension, both the Sales and Customer Support functions may be assigned to one of the resulting subunits.

In some cases, however, an org unit should be vertically divided along more than one dimension at once. For example, an entire organization may be divided into a group of org units focused on specific business functions such as Finance, Human Resources and IT, and another group of multi-functional org units focused on separate product lines or customer segments.

The design of an OS sometimes requires that choices be made for two consecutive layers at once. That is the case when a "front and back office" organizational pattern is used. The first layer of a front and back office pattern is always divided along the business function dimension. The customer-facing business functions (e.g., Call Center, Sales) are grouped together into a "front office" org unit while the Manufacturing and Delivery functions are grouped into a "back office" org unit. The second layer of a front and back office pattern can be subdivided along any of the six dimensions described above. For example, the front office org unit may be subdivided into subunits focused on individual customer segments, while the back office org unit may be subdivided into subunits focused on particular product lines.

The design of the organizational structure should include all of the horizontal org units necessary to ensure sound decision-making and effective and efficient coordination across the organization. The two most common types of horizontal org units are:

• Project team: A temporary org unit set up to create a unique product, service or other kind of result.

• Committee: An org unit made up of people from different vertical org units who are appointed to work together to make decisions on a specific matter and coordinate related activities. It may be permanent or temporary.

When members of the organization are part of a vertical org unit and one or more horizontal org units, which results in their work being supervised by more than one manager, these members are said to be managed using a matrix structure. It is important that the responsibilities of the managers in a matrix structure do not overlap. Indeed, to avoid conflicts and confusion, each member of a matrix structure must be supervised by managers who have complementary responsibilities.

When an organization has more than one business model, it should be divided into business units that each operate their own business model. This segregation allows each of the resulting business units to operate independently and execute its own strategy free of the unavoidable compromises that must be made when two or more business models are combined within a single business unit. For example, an organization engaged in both retail commerce and distribution should separate these different business models into two separate business units. The business unit that manages the retail chain should then be a customer of the business unit responsible for distribution.

An OS should not be designed based on the particular skills or preferences of existing members of the organization. Instead, it should be designed according to the leadership, coordination and skills requirements that arise from the chosen strategy. It is only once an OS has been designed that people should be assigned to positions within this structure.

In deciding how to divide an org unit into subunits, the organization structure choices made elsewhere in the organization may need to be taken into account. Consider, for example, a subunit created within the IT org unit to manage its relationships with the org units it serves throughout the organization. It may be necessary to subdivide this subunit into small teams, each of which manages the relationship with a particular org unit. In this way, the structure of the subunit matches that of the org units the IT org unit serves.

An OS should be no more and no less complex than needed. Oversimplifying an OS often results in overloaded managers who become bottlenecks in decision-making processes, which in turn significantly slows down the organization's processes. Conversely, the OS should not be unnecessarily complex, nor should it make employees' jobs more complex than a normal human being can handle.

The organization's transformation requirements must be taken into account when designing an organizational structure. When major efforts must be undertaken to transform the organization's capabilities, it is best to design an OS that frees people from other activities and allows them to focus on getting these building block transformations done right and on time.

An org unit should not be assigned a combination of business functions that puts any of its members in a position of conflict of interest. For example, an org unit whose members are rewarded for selling mortgages should not be also responsible for approving those mortgages. Hence, the design of the OS should ensure that the people who do certain work and the people who audit this work belong to different org units.

Finally, the mission statement of each org unit in the organization must be defined while the OS is being designed, not afterward. This helps to ensure that there are no responsibility gaps or overlaps in the new structure. It also helps to streamline the implementation of the OS, as managers do not have to negotiate the limits of their new responsibilities with each other once the new structure is in place. Each org unit's mission statement should be defined in a different manner than that of the whole organization. It must state what business functions, internal or external customers, geographic areas, and products or product lines, the org unit is responsible for.

Decision Rights Design Guidelines

First and foremost, the identification of the important decision types and the allocation of the associated decision rights should be spread over time. It is not practical to design the decision rights for all important decision types at once. Rather, the design should start with the most important decision types, irrespective of the organizational level at which they are made. These should include decisions that pertain to the transformation of strategic capabilities. Once these decision rights are implemented and ingrained in the culture of the organization, the decision rights for additional decision types should then be progressively specified.

The RAPID[10] framework, developed by Rogers and Blenko (2006), should be used to specify stakeholders' roles in making decisions. RAPID is similar to the RACI framework (Responsible, Accountable, Contributes, Informed), which is often used to assign deliverable responsibilities to project team members. However, RAPID is better suited for decision-making. Each of the letters in the word RAPID stands for one of the five decision roles in the framework. These roles are defined as follows:

- **R** is for Recommender. The person who has this role is responsible for gathering inputs, identifying and analyzing alternatives, and making a recommendation. That person is also responsible for getting buy-in into the recommendation to increase the likelihood that it will be approved.

- **A** is for Agree. The people who play this role have veto power over the recommendation, not the decision. The person with the **R** must therefore discuss the recommendation with the people with the **A** role before he/she can make a recommendation. In case of disagreement, the people with the **A** role must work with the recommender to develop an alternative accepted by all.

- **P** is for Perform. The people with this role are responsible for carrying out the decision once it has been made.

- **I** is for Input. The people who have this role are responsible for providing inputs used in formulating the recommendation. These same people are often involved in carrying out the decision.

- **D** is for Decide. The person who has this role is accountable for making the decision once the recommendation is made. If the people with the **R** and **A** roles cannot agree on a recommendation, the person with the **D** has the authority to resolve the impasse however he/she sees fit.

---

[10] RAPID® is a registered trademark of Bain & Company, Inc.

A few rules should be respected when assigning decision roles. First, only one person should have the *D* for each decision type unless there is more than one context. For example, with regard to sales volume discount decisions, one manager may have the *D* for the North American territory (first context) while another may have it for the European territory (second context). Second, only a few people should have the *A* role for a given decision type. If too many individuals have the power to veto a recommendation, the decision process can be paralyzed. Finally, the *I* role should be assigned only to people who can make meaningful contributions.

As a general rule, decision rights should be assigned not to specific people but to functional roles in order to minimize rework when people change positions. For example, a *D* should be assigned to the role of CEO and not to the person who occupies the CEO role.

<u>Guidelines for modeling and Documenting an Organizational Model</u>

An OM should be documented using an org chart. Tables such as the one shown in Table 3.5 should also be used to capture information about each org unit included in the OA. In addition, one or more matrices such as the one shown in Table 3.6 should be used to document decision rights.

Table 3.5: Some general information that
should be captured about each org unit

Information	Description
Name	Name of the org unit
Functions	List of functions performed by the org unit
Customers	List of customer segments or internal org units served by the org unit
Geographies	List of geographic areas served by the org unit
Manager	Name of the manager of the org unit
Parent org unit	Name of the parent org unit

Table 3.6: Generic decision rights matrix

Decision type	Positions			
	Position 1	Position 2	Position 3	Position 4
Decision type 1	R, A, P, I, or D	R, A, P, I, or D	R, A, P, I, or D	R, A, P, I, or D
Decision type 2	R, A, P, I, or D	R, A, P, I, or D	R, A, P, I, or D	R, A, P, I, or D
Decision type 3	R, A, P, I, or D	R, A, P, I, or D	R, A, P, I, or D	R, A, P, I, or D

Know-How Architecture

This section describes the key characteristics of a know-how architecture (KHA) and identifies the reasons why a KHA should be architected. It also present guidelines for architecting a KHA and for modeling and documenting a rudimentary know-how model (KHM) suitable for the needs of the business architects.[11]

Key Characteristics of a Know-How Architecture

The key things to know about a KHA:

• As implied by its name, a KHA is made up of know-how building blocks and of the relationships they have to one another.

• A KHA includes a classification scheme for the know-how held by the organization and its members. Thus, a KHA includes hierarchical relationships. In addition, it may also include peer-to-peer relationships because the creation of new knowledge often requires the combination of existing knowledge from distinct knowledge areas.

Why Design, Model and Document a Know-How Architecture?

The reasons why a KHA should be architected are:

• To help formulate the strategy. Having a current KHM can help to identify know-how, or combinations of know-how, that could be used to

---

[11] A KHM designed for knowledge management and intellectual property management purposes is usually much more complex.

create a competitive advantage. A target and current KHA also help to identify the feasibility of alternative strategies identifying the know-how gaps associated with each one.

- To identify the links between the organization's capabilities and the critical know-how they rely on. As mentioned above, a business capability always depends on specific know-how, whether patented or not.

Guidelines for Designing a Know-How Architecture

The prerequisites for designing the KHA of a slice of the organization are:

- The strategy;

- The long-term R&D plan; and

- The corresponding BCM.

Four steps are required to design a know-how classification (Lambe, 2007): (1) determine the know-how subject areas to be included; (2) collect the vocabularies; (3) draft a classification scheme; and (4) test and refine the classification scheme.

If a KHA includes a wide array of know-how, a "faceted classification" scheme should be designed (Lambe, 2007). A faceted classification is one that uses multiple classification schemes at once. For example, a consulting firm may simultaneously classify project deliverables according to their types, the projects they belong to, and the customers for whom they were prepared. The use of faceted classifications facilitates searches for know-how assets.

Guidelines for Modeling and Documenting a Know-How Model

A know-how model catalogs the organization's know-how and indicates where it can be found. However, it does not capture any of that know-how.

Organizations should build a know-how model only if it is worthwhile doing so. Building and maintaining such a model requires considerable effort and, hence, is only worthwhile for organizations whose strategic advantage depends strongly on know-how. Such organizations are usually involved in the technology, life sciences, or consulting industries and generally invest a significant portion of their budgets in research and development activities. Although other organizations also have key know-how assets, these are generally few in number and are very well known, so it is usually not worthwhile for them to build a KHM.

Many organizations for which it is worthwhile to build a KHM already have a knowledge classification and/or IP catalog. Business architects should leverage those whenever possible instead of building their KHM from scratch.

If it is worthwhile to build a KHM but no knowledge classification or IP catalog exists, the most critical know-how items to be included in the model are the organization's IP and the know-how tied to strategic capabilities. Patents and know-how related to the product and service R&D, marketing and sales functions are generally a good place to start.

Some of the general information to be captured about each know-how asset included in a KHM is shown in Table 3.7.

In our practice, we like to document a KHM using a city map diagram. Figure 3.17 presents an example of a high-level knowledge city map diagram for a number of engineering disciplines.

Business Information Architecture

This section describes the key characteristics of a business information architecture (BIA) and identifies the reasons why a BIA should be architected. It also presents guidelines for designing a BIA and for modeling and documenting its corresponding business information model (BIM).

Table 3.7: Some general information to be captured
about each know-how asset included in a KHM

Information	Description
Name	Name of the know-how asset
Description	Description of the know-how asset
Type	Type of know-how asset (Intellectual capital, Intellectual asset or Intellectual property)
State	Life cycle state of the know-how asset (Current*/Gap**/In development***)
Legal owner	Legal owner of the capability (in the case of intellectual property)
Location	Where the know-how asset can be found (in a particular person's head, in a document, in a patent or in a database)

* Know-how asset that currently exists within the organization.
** Know-how asset that the organization needs but does not currently hold.
*** Know-how asset currently being developed.

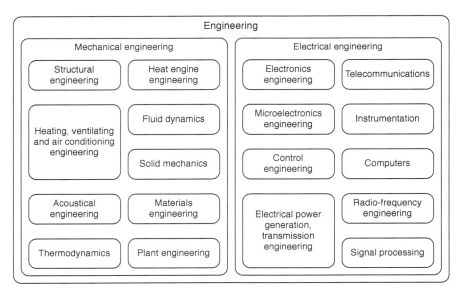

Figure 3.17: High-level knowledge city map
diagram for several engineering disciplines

Key Characteristics of an Information Architecture

The key things to know about a BIA:

- A BIA is made up of concepts and the relationships they have to one another. Each concept represents a type of "thing" (e.g., customer) about which the organization can gather information (e.g., customer's name, address, date of birth) and is referred to using a business term. Examples of such concepts include Customer, Product, Transaction, Supplier, Role, Employee, Customer interaction and Address.

- The relationships in the BIA indicate how concepts are related to one another. These relationships are named using verbs (e.g., a Customer places an Order). A BIA includes both hierarchical relationships and peer-to-peer relationships. A hierarchical relationship can be of either the classification or decomposition type. For example, the concepts of Person and Enterprise are classified under the concept of Party while Figure 3.1 decomposes the atomic capability concept into the concepts underlying each of the eight types of base building blocks of which a atomic capability is made up. A peer-to-peer relationship represents any other type of relationship concepts may have to another (e.g., a Process is made of Tasks).

Why Design, Model and Document a Business Information Architecture?

The reasons why a BIA should be architected are:

- To create a glossary of business terms, and to understand how these terms relate to each other in order to facilitate and clarify communication between members of the organization.

- To clearly identify the information required by the organization's processes, and the activities they are made up of.

- To identify the information that the organization's information systems need to manage. Information systems architects rely on the BIM to design the data structures used by the organization's information systems.

• To be able to structure information access privileges in accordance with people's functional roles within the organization.

Guidelines for Designing a Business Information Architecture

The prerequisites for designing the BIA of a slice of the organization are:

• The strategy; and

• The corresponding BCM.

When the same business term is used to refer to different concepts or, conversely, when different terms are used to refer to a single concept, business architects should work with the people who use these business terms to standardize and harmonize the terminology. To illustrate this, let us take the example of a mobile phone service company. Its retail business unit, which sells phones and provides services to the general public, uses the term "customer" to refer to a person paying for the service. However, the business unit operating the mobile phone network uses the term "customer" to refer to any individual using a mobile phone connected to the company's network (including employees who are given a mobile phone free of charge). To eliminate possible confusion, the term "customer" should be replaced by the terms "retail customer" and "network customer."

The BIA should be designed by business architects who are very good at grasping business concepts and their relationships. If the business architects have not yet developed BIA design skills, they should seek the help of IT enterprise data architects. In cases where no IT enterprise data architect is available, business architects may rely on the support of database administrators. However, this should be done with great care because the fact that a person has good database administration technical skills does not guarantee in any way that he/she has the conceptual skills required to help design a BIA.

Guidelines for Modeling and Documenting a Business Information Model

The BIM should include a definition of each concept it includes. These definitions should be documented in a corporate glossary.

In our practice, we like to document a BIM using city map diagrams, concept maps and a glossary of business terms. A concept map identifies the business terms used in a particular context (e.g., business function) and the relationships that exist between them. A very simple example of a concept map is shown in Figure 3.18. Evidently, a real concept map for a customer order would be more complex.

Brand Architecture

This section describes the key characteristics of a brand architecture and identifies the reasons why a brand architecture should be designed, modeled and documented. It also presents rudimentary guidelines for designing a brand architecture and for modeling and documenting the corresponding brand model.

Key Characteristics of a Brand Architecture

The key things to know about a brand architecture:

- A brand architecture is made up of brands and sub-brands (e.g., Dove Purely Pampering and Dove Go Fresh are sub-brands of Dove[12]).

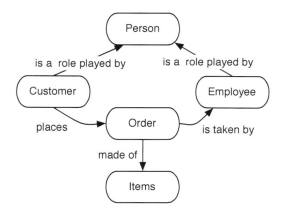

Figure 3.18: Sample concept map

---

[12] Dove, Dove Purely Pampering and Dove Go Fresh are registered trademarks of Unilever.

Hence, a brand architecture includes hierarchical relationships of the classification type.

- A brand architecture also identifies and describes the key customer value proposition attributes shared by the products and/or services sold under each brand and sub-brand (i.e., brand attributes).

Why Design, Model and Document a Brand Architecture?

The reasons why a brand architecture should be designed, modeled and documented are:

- A well-designed brand architecture enables the organization to easily communicate to its customers the identity of its products and services (e.g., Tide detergent), and of the customer value proposition associated with each of these products and services.

- The brand architecture is a key input to the design of the other sub-architectures of the TBA. Indeed, the customer value proposition associated with each brand can greatly influence not only the design of the products and/or services sold under each brand but also the design of the capabilities that enable the design, manufacturing, marketing, sales and after-sales support of these same products and services.

Guidelines for Designing a Brand Architecture

The prerequisites for designing the brand architecture are:

- The strategy

- The long-term R&D plan; and

- The customer segment, location, and products and services context perspectives (described later in this chapter);

Each brand's customer value proposition must be aligned with the strategy's customer value proposition (Figure 3.19). In fact, the design of each brand's attributes should be bounded by the price/cost, availability, quality, functionality, service, partnership and image attributes formulated in the customer value proposition of the organization's strategy. The set of attributes designed into each brand should thus further refine the customer value proposition formulated in the organization's strategy. For example, a high-end cosmetics company may have a brand of high-end hypoallergenic products and a brand of high-end environmentally friendly products but not a brand of cheap low-quality products.

Moreover, *"it only makes sense to have multiple brands within a [product or service] category if each of them can be positioned against a unique [customer] segment."* (Kumar and Steenkamp, 2007, p. 190). Indeed, having multiple brands within a category targeting the same customer segments makes it hard to create and maintain the reputation of each of these brands and increases both manufacturing and marketing costs.

Guidelines for Modeling and Documenting a Brand Model

A diagram showing each of the organization's brands and sub-brands should be drawn (see Figure 3.20 for an example). This diagram should include the names and logos of each brand and sub-brand.

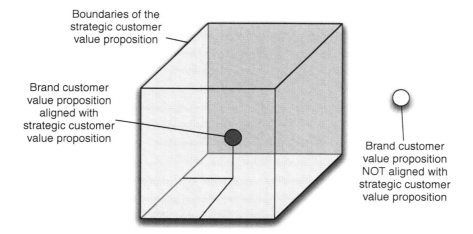

Figure 3.19: Aligning the brand's customer value proposition with the strategy's customer value proposition

Some of the general information to be captured about each brand and sub-brand included in a brand architecture is shown in Table 3.8.

Designing, Modeling and Documenting Composite Architectures

Architecting one or a few slices of an organization requires, in addition to the design of homogeneous architectures, the design of several composite architectures (i.e., architectures that specify relationships between building blocks of different types). Regarding the guidelines that pertain to these composite architectures, we will limit our discussion to the following two points. First, business architects should carefully select which composite architectures they design and model. Out of the multitude of possible options, only a few are likely to add value to the organization in any given context. In addition, the more composite architectures are designed and modeled, the more likely it is that they will not be maintained and thus will become obsolete.

Second, there are two main ways to document a composite model. The first is to use a diagram that shows a number of building blocks of different types and the relationships that exist between them. Numerous types of such diagrams can be drawn. The type to be used depends on

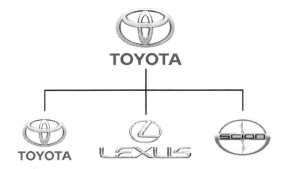

Figure 3.20: Example brand architecture diagram
(Toyota, Lexus and Scion are trademarks of Toyota)

Table 3.8: Some general information to be captured
about each brand included in a brand model

Attribute	Description
Name	Name of the brand
Type	Brand or sub-brand
Parent brand (if sub-brand)	Name of the parent brand (if the brand is a sub-brand)
Logo	Logo of the brand
Brand attributes	Key attributes that distinguish the products and services tagged with this brand from similar products and services tagged with other brands
Target customer segments	Customer segments for whom the products and services tagged with this brand are destined
Target locations	Geographic regions where the products and services tagged with this brand are to be sold

the message to be conveyed. Examples of such diagrams are shown in Figures 3.21, 3.22 and 3.23. The second way to document composite models is to use matrices and tables. Each matrix or table is used to document a particular type of relationship. An example of a matrix showing the information created or used by different processes is shown in Figure 3.24.

Three Key Perspectives of the Organizational Context

In addition to architecting the TBA, business architects must often model and document three key perspectives of the target organizational context: the organization's products and services, its locations, and its customer segments. Strictly speaking, the models of these three organizational context perspectives are not business architecture models and, as such, should ideally be built by other professionals (i.e., not business architects) in the organization who are accountable for their content. However, because these context models are required inputs to the TBA architecture

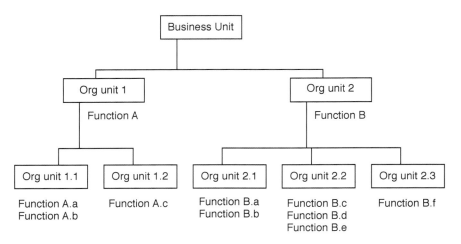

Figure 3.21: Template of a diagram showing the business functions performed by different org units

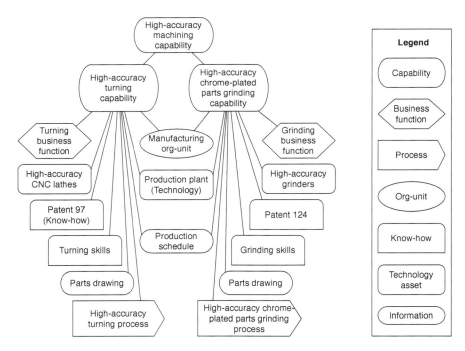

Figure 3.22: Diagram showing the building blocks the Machine Highly Accurate Metal Parts capability is made up of

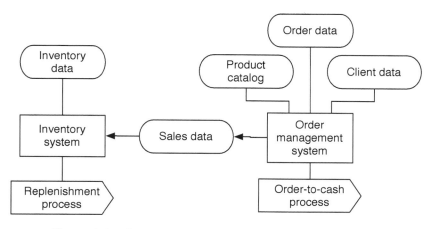

Figure 3.23: Sample diagram showing the relationships between information systems, information groups and processes

Processes \ Information	Business case	Cascaded objectives	Communicated strategy	Current architecture	Feedback from Define trans. plan	Feedback from Execute project	Feedback from Execute trans. plan	Incentives	Awarded incentives	Long-term financial plan	Project authorization	Project cost actuals and forecast	Project definition	Progress reports	Rolling financial forecast	Scorecard	Strategy	Strategic assumptions	Target architecture	Transformation	Transformation plan
Form strategy			I													I	O				
Build long-term financial plan										O					I			I			
Define target architecture			I	I												I	I		O		
Define transformation plan	I						I									I	I		I		O
Communicate strategy			O														I				
Build business case	O		I										I				I				
Execute transformation plan						I					O			I	I						I
Update rolling financial forecast											I		I		O						I
Execute project			I								I	O	O						I	O	
Cascade objectives and incentives		O						O										I			I
Publish scorecard	I												I		I	O					
Award incentives								I	O							I					
Document current architecture				O																	

Legend I: Input O: Output

Figure 3.24: Example of a matrix showing the information used and created by several processes

process and because they are often not available, business architects must frequently take the lead in modeling and documenting them in collaboration with the people who are accountable for their final content.

This section defines the three key perspectives of the organizational context and identifies why they should be modeled and documented. It also presents guidelines for modeling and documenting these perspectives of the organizational context.

Definition of the Three Context Perspectives

The key things to know about the three perspectives of the organizational context are:

- The products and services perspective identifies the products and services the organization sells and the key products and services it purchases.

- The location perspective includes all the regions of the world where the organization manufactures, sells or purchases products and services. It also includes the land, plants and other buildings from which the organization operates.

- The customer segment perspective includes all of the customer segments defined by the organization. A customer segment is a subset of the organization's clientele which is made up of customers who share similar characteristics that are of interest to the organization (e.g., they live in the same geographic area, are in the same age group, have similar needs or tastes).

Why Model and Document the Three Perspectives

Models of these three perspectives of the organizational context are required so business architects can model and document the relationships that exist between:

- Processes and the products and services they consume and create;

- Org units and the products and services they produce;

- Org units and the customer segments they serve;

- Org units and the geographic areas they serve;

- Locations and technology assets or natural resource deposits;

- Products and services and the sales territories in which they will be sold; and

- Locations and the applicable laws and standards within each one.

Guidelines for Modeling and Documenting the Context Perspectives

Modeling the products and services perspective is a two-step process: (1) define the classification scheme; and (2) classify the products and services within it. It is very common for the classification scheme to be structured as illustrated in Figure 3.25. That is, product and service lines are subdivided into categories which are themselves subdivided into groups of individual products and services.

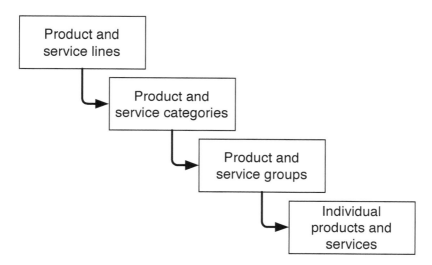

Figure 3.25: Typical structure of a products and services classification scheme

The location perspective model often divides the surface of the globe in several ways at once to serve different needs. The two most common are:

- A successive subdivision of continents into countries, states, counties, and cities where the organization operates, buys or sells.

- A subdivision into sales territories. For example, an organization may decide to organize its North American sales team around Eastern, Central and Western sales regions that are each made up of U.S. states and Canadian provinces.

The customer segment perspective model defines the customer segments used by the organization. Organizations often use different types of customer segmentation simultaneously (e.g., geographic, demographic and value segments); as a result, a given customer can belong to multiple segments at the same time.

The products and services, location and customer segment models can each be documented using a simple catalog.

Relationships Between the Concepts at the Heart of the Target Business Architecture

Figure 3.26 presents all of the relationships that exist between the different types of building blocks, strategy components, goals and constraints, as well as components of the three key perspectives of the organizational context used when designing, modeling and documenting the TBA.

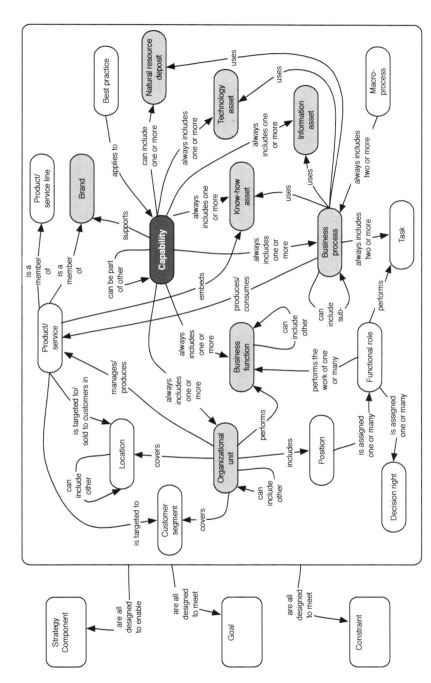

Figure 3.26: Relationships between the different types of building blocks, strategy components, goals, constraints and components of the three perspectives of the organizational context

References

Barros, O. (2007) Business Process Architecture and Design. *BPTrends*, May.

Blackler, F. (1995) Knowledge, Knowledge Work and Organizations: An Overview and Interpretation. *Organization Studies*, 16(6), 1021-1046.

Blenko, M.W., and Davis-Peccoud, J. (2011) *Great Decisions – Not a Solo Performance*. Bain & Company, Boston.

Blenko, M.W., Mankins, M.C., and Rogers, P. (2010) *Decide and Deliver: 5 Steps to Breakthrough Performance in Your Organization*. Harvard Business School Publishing, Boston.

Egbu, C.O. (2004) Managing Knowledge and Intellectual Capital for Improved Organizational Innovations in the Construction Industry: An Examination of Critical Success Factors. *Engineering, Construction and Architectural Management*, 11(5), 301-315.

Galbraith, J.R. (2002) *Designing Organizations: An Executive Guide to Strategy, Structure, and Process*. Jossey-Bass, San Francisco.

Grant, R.M. (1991) The Resource-Based Theory of Competitive Advantage: Implications for Strategy Formulation. *California Management Review*, Spring, 114-135.

Hammer, M., and Champy, J. (2006) *Reengineering the Corporation: Manifesto for Business Revolution*. Harper Business, New York.

Harmon, P. (2003) *Business Process Change: A Manager's Guide to Improving, Redesigning, and Automating Processes*. Morgan Kaufmann Publishers, San Francisco.

Kates, A., and Galbraith, J. R. (2007) *Designing Your Organization: Using the STAR Model to Solve 5 Critical Design Challenges*. John Wiley & Sons, San Francisco.

Kumar, N. and, Steenkamp, J.-B.E.M. (2007) *Private Label Strategy*. Harvard Business School Publishing, Boston.

Lam, A. (2000) Tacit Knowledge, Organizational Learning and Societal Institutions: An Integrated Framework. *Organization Studies*, 21(3), 487-513.

Lambe, P. (2007) *Organizing Knowledge: Taxonomies, Knowledge and Organizational Effectiveness*. Chandos Publishing, Oxford.

Makadok, R. (2001) Toward a Synthesis of the Resource-Based View and Dynamic-Capability Views of Rent Creation. *Strategic Management Journal*, 22(5), 387-401.

McConnachie, G. (1997) The Management of Intellectual Assets: Delivering Value to the Business. *Journal of Knowledge Management*, 1(1), 56-62.

Mintzberg, H. (1979) *The Structuring of Organizations: A Synthesis of the Research*. Prentice-Hall, Englewood Cliffs, NJ.

Nunes, P.F., and Breene T. (2011) *Strategy at the Edge*. Accenture Outlook, June.

Object Management Group (2008) *Business Process Maturity Model (BPMM) version 1.0*.

Rogers, P., and Blenko, M. (2006) Who Has the D? How Clear Decision Roles Enhance Organizational Performance. *Harvard Business Review*, January, 52-61.

Silver, B. (2011) *BPMN Method & Style with BPMN Implementer's Guide*, Second Edition. Cody-Cassidy Press, Aptos, CA.

Sullivan, P.H. (1999) Profiting from Intellectual Capital. *Journal of Knowledge Management*, 3(2), 132-142.

Teece, D.J., Pisano, G., and Shuen, A. (1997) Dynamic Capabilities and Strategic Management. *Strategic Management Journal*, 18(7), 509-533.

Chapter 4

Elaborating the Transformation Plan

Business architects play a critical role in the elaboration of the transformation plan (TP). A TP identifies and sequences the transformation projects that the organization must execute to implement parts or all of its target enterprise architecture (TEA). It is based on a comparison between the current enterprise architecture (CEA) and TEA to identify the building block transformations that must be executed to improve the organization's ability to execute its strategy[1]. The TP should encompass all of the slices of the organization that have been architected so far. Because it can take a decade or more for an organization to implement its TEA in full and because things invariably change along the way, at any point in time the TP should cover only the next three to five years of the strategy implementation. The elaboration of the TP should

---

[1] To lighten the text throughout this chapter and the next, we will minimize our use of the words "transformation" and "building block" when talking about transformation projects and building block transformations by simply referring to them as projects and transformations, respectively.

account for the need to continuously improve the organization's financial performance; the extended organization's capacity and readiness to transform itself; the need to build and maintain momentum throughout the implementation of the strategy; and the strategic importance, dependencies, benefits, costs, elapsed time to completion, assumptions and risks associated with each building block transformation.

The objective of this chapter is to describe what constitutes a sound TP, and describe why and how to elaborate such a plan. The first section identifies the reasons why organizations should elaborate a TP. In the second section, we describe the key characteristics of a sound TP. The third section presents the shortcomings of the traditional approach used to elaborate a TP, while the fourth section describes the target-architecture-based methodology[2] we have devised to overcome these shortcomings and the techniques[3] upon which it is based. The fifth and last section presents the relationships that exist between the various concepts at the heart of a sound TP.

This chapter is primarily intended for readers who want to contribute to the challenging effort of elaborating their organization's TP. Readers who only wish to gain a high-level understanding of how to elaborate a sound TP can limit themselves to reading the first three sections and the introduction to the fourth section of this chapter.

Why Elaborate a Transformation Plan?

The reasons why an organization should elaborate a TP are:

•   To identify the best set of projects and appropriately sequence their execution to implement parts or all of its TEA and enhance its ability to execute its strategy. The TP identifies the best transformation projects

---

[2]   We define "methodology" as a formalized, repeatable series of activities performed to address a particular type of problem (adapted from Open Group, 2009–2011).

[3]   We define "technique" as a set of specific steps for completing one or some of the activities of a methodology.

based on their benefits, resource requirements (e.g., financial and human resources), risks and, most importantly, whether or not they are essential to the implementation of the strategy (i.e., projects that make major contributions to the owner, customer, partner and employee value propositions, or that are prerequisites for such projects). Furthermore, elaborating the TP enables the organization to optimize the sequencing of transformation projects by taking into account the dependencies between them. This reduces the likelihood of omitting prerequisite transformations and having to perform expensive rework.

- To avoid priority proliferation by modulating the execution of the essential transformations in accordance with the readiness and capacity of the extended organization (i.e., the organization and its close partners) to transform itself. The TP can therefore help the organization overcome *"the common tendency to take on too much and then do everything 'Just OK',"* which is one of biggest barriers to successful strategy implementation according to Zagotta and Robinson (2002, p. 32).

- To maximize the synergies, coherence and coordination between transformation projects during the execution of the TP. By identifying all of the interrelationships (shared objectives, building blocks and/or prerequisite transformations) that exist between different projects, a sound TP makes it much easier to take these interrelationships into consideration when making decisions during the execution of the TP. For example, the teams working on two projects that need similar software may work together to select a single software package that meets the requirements of both projects.

- To enable effective monitoring of the progress made while executing the TP. In addition to allowing the organization to compare its progress to a plan and to identify where corrective actions are needed, the TP can also ensure that this comparison is made with a solid baseline.

The Key Characteristics of a Sound Transformation Plan

To provide the organization with the benefits identified above, the TP must have four key characteristics. First, 11 key factors must be taken into account during the elaboration of the TP (Figure 4.1). Four of these are key inputs to the TP elaboration process. Indeed, a sound TP is aligned with the strategy, is based on a comparison between the CEA and TEA and complies with applicable regulations. The other seven factors are

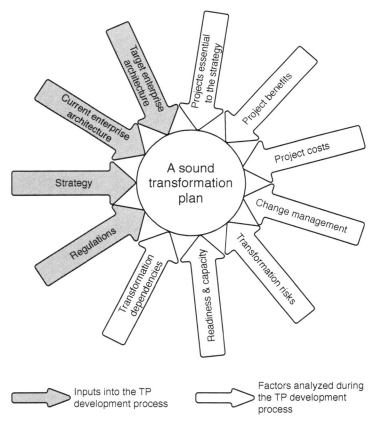

Figure 4.1: Key factors that must be taken into account during the elaboration of the TP

analyzed during the TP elaboration process. Indeed, a sound TP selects and sequences projects based on whether they are essential or optional to the implementation of the strategy, their anticipated benefits, their resource requirements, the dependencies that exist between the transformations, the transformation risks, and the extended organization's readiness and capacity to transform itself. In addition, a sound TP is devised to facilitate change management.

Second, a sound TP should include all building block transformations that must be executed to improve the organization's ability to execute its strategy. Indeed, for the TP to be executable, it should include not only the transformations that will need to be made to business architecture building blocks (i.e., capabilities, processes, functions, org units, know-how assets, information assets and brands) but also those that will need to be made to technology asset and natural resource deposit building blocks. For example, the transformation of a business process may require new know-how assets, new information assets, a new information system, and the creation of a new org unit that will perform a new function.

Third, the elaboration of a sound TP requires the use of a methodology that fosters the objective analysis of the 11 factors identified above and generates the evidence needed for sound decision-making. The methodology used should also promote the use of predefined decision criteria to ensure that the proposed TP is the best path to transform the organization and get stakeholders to accept that some of their own projects will have to be postponed in favor of other projects. For best results, the methodology and decision criteria should be discussed and agreed upon by key stakeholders at the onset of the TP elaboration process.

Fourth, a sound TP should comprise the following documents:

• Enterprise Architecture Gap Analysis: A document that describes the gaps between the CEA and TEA. Multiple gaps may exist between a building block's current and target states. For example, there may be both a quality gap and an operational risk gap between a process's current and target states.

- Result Chain of the TP: A cognitive map, or "mind map," that graphically represents a shared understanding of what transformations must be undertaken, and in what order, to move the organization towards its target state and achieve its goals (adapted from IT Governance Institute, 2008).

- Project Business Cases: A set of documents each of which explains the pros and cons of executing the transformations within the scope of a particular project. In addition to determining whether a given project is essential or optional to the implementation of the strategy, a business case should identify the objectives, tangible and intangible benefits, resource requirements (e.g., financial, human, technology and non-technology assets) and risks, and the extended organization's readiness and capacity to execute this project.

- Business Transformation Readiness and Capacity Management Plan: A document that identifies the readiness and capacity challenges the extended organization will face in executing the TP and the means by which these challenges can be overcome.

- Business Transformation Risk Management Plan: A document that describes the overall risks inherent to the execution of the TP and identifies the means by which these risks can be mitigated.

- Business Transformation Assumption Analysis: A short document that identifies key assumptions together with the impacts they may have if proven false and, when necessary, the means by which they should be verified.

- Project Prioritization Analysis: A complementary document to the roadmap that summarizes the information and logic used to select, prioritize and sequence the transformation projects. This document should identify the projects that are essential to the implementation of the strategy and those that are optional. This document should also identify how the benefits and resource requirements of each project, the dependencies that exist between the transformations, the transformation risks, and the extended organization's readiness and capacity to execute the TP were used to prioritize and sequence the transformation projects.

- Project/Program Charters [4]: A set of documents each of which identifies the purpose and scope of a particular project/program; as a whole, they identify the scope of the TP. Each charter should identify the project/program sponsor and the set of transformation work packages/ projects included in a given project/program.

- Roadmap: A document that shows, on a timeline, when each of the transformation projects and programs is planned to be executed. This document only identifies the critical milestones of each project and program (e.g., start, finish) and hence does not include a detailed plan of each project.

- Business Transformation Plan Executive Summary: A brief document that summarizes the content of the above set of documents.

These documents are the outputs from the target-architecture-based methodology we propose later in this chapter.

Problems with the Traditional Approach to Defining the Transformation Plan

Project Portfolio Management (PPM) is used by organizations to define and manage the portfolio of projects that make up their TP. According to the Project Management Institute (2008), PPM is the coordinated

---

[4] A program is "*a group of related projects, subprograms, and program activities that are managed in a coordinated way to obtain benefits not available from managing them individually*" (Project Management Institute, 2008, p. 139).

management of a set of projects grouped together to facilitate the achievement of selected business objectives. It is concerned with ensuring that the organization is *"doing the right projects"* rather than *"doing projects right"* (Project Management Institute, 2008, p. 6). PPM is used to identify, select, prioritize, govern and monitor projects and to report on their contributions and their relative alignment with the organization's objectives.

The traditional approach to PPM starts with the identification of the projects that are relevant to a particular portfolio[5] and the preparation of a business case for each one. The projects are then individually rated using a scoring model composed of weighted criteria such as strategic alignment, tangible and intangible benefits, and costs. The resulting scores are then used to compare the projects with each other in order to select and prioritize those that will remain in the portfolio. Graphical analytical methods such as the bubble graph shown in Figure 4.2 are used to select and prioritize the projects. This traditional approach is generally applied once or twice a year and orchestrated by a project portfolio manager under the supervision of an executive or a committee.

The traditional approach to PPM has substantial merit in that it considers many more factors than simply return on investment to select and prioritize projects. However, the approach has three important shortcomings when used to elaborate a TP. First, the traditional approach to PPM lacks a critical input, the TEA. Instead of relying on the TEA to identify transformation projects, the PPM approach relies on the annual or biannual submission of project proposals, generally conceived in silos by leaders across the organization seeking to improve the performance of their own areas. This way of identifying projects often makes the resulting TP a haphazard mix of overlapping projects that contribute little or nothing to the implementation of the strategy and whose sequencing does not

---

5   Large organizations often have five types of project portfolios: (1) fundamental research; (2) product and service development; (3) maintenance; (4) evolution; and (5) transformation. This chapter discusses only the fifth type.

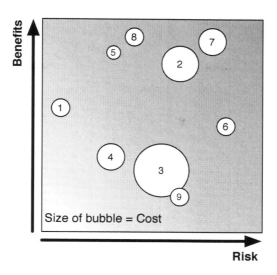

Figure 4.2: Sample bubble graph

account for the dependencies between projects. That is, projects that do not contribute to the implementation of the strategy and may even hinder its execution are often proposed and selected while others that are critical to the execution of the strategy may never even be proposed.

Second, the traditional approach to PPM does not attribute enough importance to the "strategic alignment" criterion during the selection and prioritization of projects. Indeed, each project's contributions to the implementation of the strategy are put on an equal footing with other criteria such as financial benefits, costs and risks. This lack of attention to each project's contribution to the implementation of the strategy and the over-reliance on the scoring method often results in essential projects being eliminated from the TP in favor of projects that contribute little or nothing to the strategy but get higher scores because they provide higher short-term financial benefits and have lower risks. Unfortunately, this issue is very difficult to resolve, even by better weighting each criterion in the scoring model. In fact, we have never been able to devise a scoring model that reliably ensures that all projects that are essential to the implementation of the strategy are prioritized over other projects, nor have we ever encountered anybody who did. However, we have seen organizations that, once they realized that their initial scoring model did not prioritize the right projects, adjusted the weights and scores until their preferred projects got the highest scores.

Third, the traditional approach to PPM does not put enough emphasis on the dependencies between transformations when selecting and prioritizing projects. Instead of relying on a rigorous technique to account for all of the dependencies between transformations, the approach considers only the most obvious dependencies during project selection and prioritization. Without a solid understanding of all transformation dependencies, prerequisite projects, which can have lower scores than other projects, are often discarded, thus creating holes in the foundations required to execute the remaining projects. These holes, often discovered only once project execution is under way, generate cost overruns and force unwanted adjustments to ongoing projects. Furthermore, because financial commitments have now been made and project deadlines have been set, more often than not these holes are filled with what can be best described as patches instead of proper foundations for the future. Worse yet, these patches may eventually need to be replaced at significant costs. In addition to increasing the time and costs required to execute projects, neglecting to consider the dependencies that exist between transformations is likely to have a negative impact on the quality of the transformations executed and thus hinder the execution of the strategy.

Target Architecture-Based Methodology to Create the Transformation Plan

As discussed in the previous section, the traditional approach to PPM has three important shortcomings that are often detrimental to the implementation of the strategy. This section describes in detail the target-architecture-based methodology and related techniques that we recommend to overcome these shortcomings and increase the likelihood of successfully implementing a strategy. This methodology comprises 10 phases whose purpose can be summarized as follows:

- Initiation (P_1): Structure the elaboration of the TP as a project;

- Transformation Work Packages (P_2): Identify the gaps between the organization's CEA and TEA (i.e., identify the building block transformations that must be executed), define goals related to the filling of these gaps and define transformation work packages to achieve these goals;

- Initial Result Chain (P_3): Map on a result chain the previously identified work packages together with their dependencies and the goals they contribute to;

- Readiness and Capacity (P_4): Analyze the extended organization's readiness and capacity to execute the TP and add to the result chain the work packages needed to resolve the significant capacity and readiness challenges identified;

- Key Assumptions (P_5): Identify the key assumptions underlying the strategy, the TEA and the TP, and add to the result chain the work packages whose purpose will be to verify these assumptions as soon as possible;

- Risks (P_6): Identify and analyze the risks associated with each work package and devise means of mitigating them. Some of these means may take the form of additional work packages that will need to be added to the map;

- Project Identification and Analysis (P_7): Bundle related work packages together to form projects, build a business case for each project, and use these business cases to determine which of these projects are essential or optional to the implementation of the strategy and to score and rank the projects;

- TP Backbone (P_8): Create the backbone of the TP by sequencing the projects identified as essential to the execution of the strategy and optimize this backbone by identifying and resolving the significant issues it may have;

- Optional projects (P_9): Select optional projects based on their scores and dependencies and add them to the roadmap to take advantage of any transformation capacity that may remain; and,

- Finalization (P_{10}): Finalize the TP and get it approved.

The Techniques

This section describes the eight techniques at the heart of our target-architecture-based methodology: enterprise architecture gap analysis, result chain mapping, business transformation readiness and capacity analysis, business transformation risk analysis, business case analysis, scoring and ranking analysis, roadmapping, and transformation plan optimization. These techniques are presented in the order in which they are used in the methodology.

Enterprise Architecture Gap Analysis

The enterprise architecture gap analysis technique is used to identify the gaps between the current and target states of each enterprise architecture building block. Because capabilities can only be transformed by transforming their constituent building blocks, it is important that this analysis identifies and describes the gaps at the level of the building blocks. The results of the enterprise architecture gap analysis should be presented as shown in Table 4.1. The following information should be captured for each gap: (1) the name of the building block that needs to be transformed; (2) the type of building block it is; (3) the name of its parent capability; (4) a description of the gap including whether it entails the acquisition/creation, modification or sale/retirement of the building block; (5) the reasons why the gap must be filled; and (6) whether or not filling this gap is essential to the execution of the strategy.

Table 4.1: Enterprise architecture gap analysis

Building block name	Type of building block	Parent capability	Description of the gap	Motivation	Essential to the implementation of the strategy?
Capability A	Atomic capability	Capability B	Description of what needs to be modified in this capability	Why should this base capability be transformed?	Yes or No
Process C	Process	Capability A	Description of what needs to be modified in this process	Why should this gap be filled?	...
IT System D	Technology asset	Capability A	Description of what needs to be modified in this IT system	Why should this IT system be transformed?	...
Capability E	Atomic capability	Capability F	...	...	...
Process G	Process	Capability E	...	...	...
Function H	Function	Capability E	...	...	...
Information J	Information asset	Capability E	...	...	...
...	...		...	...	...

Result Chain Mapping

The result chain mapping technique was introduced by John Thorp and Fujitsu Consulting in a book called *The Information Paradox* (1998). It is a technique used to map the linkage that exists between an organization's initiatives and related goals[6] and assumptions. According to the IT Governance Institute (2008), a result chain is a cognitive map or "mind map" that graphically represents a shared understanding of how goals will be achieved in a particular context. More specifically, the result chain is used to create a map that links the organization's initiatives to the goals they contribute to, the assumptions that must hold true for these goals to

---

[6] Although Fujitsu Consulting and Thorp (1998) use the term "outcome," we prefer to use the word "goal" to maintain uniform language throughout this book.

be attainable, and the goals that must be attained before these initiatives can be successfully executed. Such a map clearly identifies the dependencies between initiatives and how each initiative ultimately contributes to the strategic goals. Figure 4.3 depicts a simple example of a result chain.

A result chain is made up of four kinds of elements (Fujitsu Consulting and Thorp, 1998). Applied to our context:

1. As described in Chapter 2, goals are of two main types: transformation and continuance. Only transformation goals (i.e., goals that require transformations to be attained) need to be mapped on a result chain. A goal is represented by an ellipse in a result chain. We like to graphically differentiate between four sub-types of transformation goals, as shown in Figure 4.4: (1) transformation facilitation goals (e.g., mitigation of a transformation risk, building a readiness and transformation capacity); (2) gap remediation goals

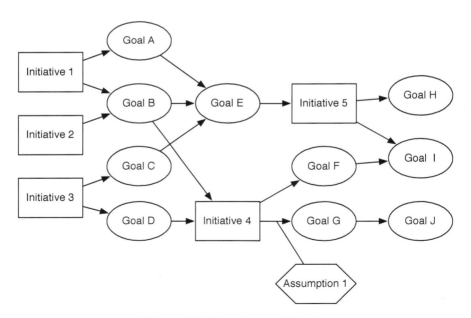

Figure 4.3: Sample result chain

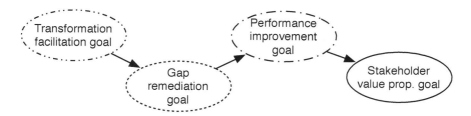

Figure 4.4: The four sub-types of transformation goals

(e.g., Process XYZ redesigned); (3) performance improvement goals (e.g., "Less than 0.2% of parts reworked"); and (4) stakeholder value proposition goals (see Chapter 2). Transformation facilitation goals are prerequisites for gap remediation goals, which are prerequisites for performance improvement goals, which in turn are prerequisites for stakeholder value proposition goals.

2. Initiatives are planned actions undertaken to contribute to one or more goals. An initiative is represented by a rectangle in a result chain. As shown in Figure 4.5, an initiative can be a work package, a project or a program. A work package contributes to the transformation of one base building block or facilitates one or more transformations (e.g., mitigate a risk, build transformation readiness). Projects comprise one or more work packages, while programs are made up

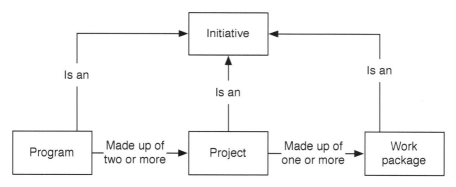

Figure 4.5: Types of initiatives

of two or more projects. When creating the TP, a result chain is first drawn at the level of the work packages, then summarized at the project level and finally, if need be, at the program level.

3. The arrows between initiatives and goals in a result chain represent contributions. As shown in Figure 4.6, a given initiative contributes to the attainment of one or more goals while the attainment of a goal can contribute to the attainment of one or more additional goals or may be a prerequisite to one or more additional initiatives. An initiative can never contribute directly to another initiative. Indeed, as shown in Figure 4.7, an initiative can only contribute to another initiative by going through at least one goal. By mapping contributions in this way, the result chain provides a good understanding of the dependencies that exist between initiatives and goals.

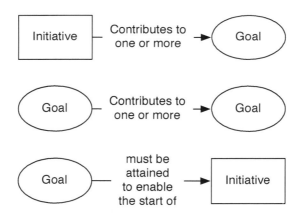

Figure 4.6: Linkages between initiatives and goals

Figure 4.7: Linkages between Initiatives

4. Assumptions are things accepted as true without proof and over which the organization has little or no control, but which, if proven false, can lead to the invalidation, in part or in whole, of the strategy, TEA or TP. An assumption is represented by a hexagon in a result chain. As shown in Figure 4.8, an assumption can be of three types: (1) that a given initiative will contribute to a given goal (assumption 1); (2) that the achievement of a given goal will contribute to the achievement of another particular goal (assumption 2); or (3) that a given goal can be achieved (assumptions 3 and 4). Because making assumptions is unavoidable during the formulation of the strategy, the creation of the TEA and TP, and because some of these assumptions can have significant negative impacts if proven false, it is essential to identify and map the important ones in the result chain and, when possible, define initiatives to validate them as soon as possible during the execution of the TP. Indeed, the insights obtained by verifying these assumptions may lead to significant improvements in the TP, the TEA and ultimately the strategy.

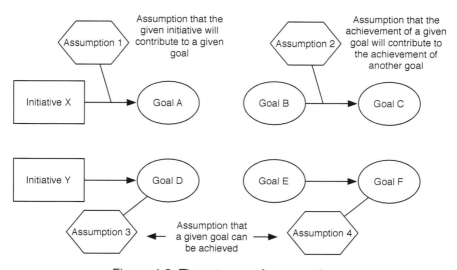

Figure 4.8: Three types of assumptions

The process of developing a result chain map promotes discussion and consensus while bringing about commitment and acceptance by executives (Fujitsu Consulting and Thorp, 1998; IT Governance Institute, 2008). It also develops a shared understanding of the dependencies that exist between the initiatives and the goals they aim to attain. Understanding this linkage, in turn, allows stakeholders to more realistically assess how and when each goal can be achieved.

Business Transformation Readiness and Capacity Analysis

Organizations that aspire to transform themselves may find themselves, or their partners, unprepared or lacking capacity in certain areas. For example, a particular kind of expertise may be in too short supply. To identify these readiness and capacity challenges, we recommend performing a Business Transformation Readiness and Capacity Analysis (BTRCA). The purpose of such an analysis is to identify the readiness and capacity factors that influence the successful transformation of the extended organization (e.g., financial resources, expertise, buy-in), analyze these factors to determine whether there are gaps between their current and required states and, if there are, describe those gaps. The BTRCA should focus on identifying and describing gaps that will require significant efforts to resolve; there is no need to focus on gaps that can be resolved by simple actions. In addition, the BTRCA should identify, analyze and describe gaps that apply to the TP as a whole, are common to multiple projects, or need to be managed long before the start of some projects. Performing a BTRCA does not eliminate the need to perform a more detailed project/program-specific readiness and capacity analysis at the start of each project/program. In fact, the BTRCA should serve as an input to each project/program's readiness and capacity analysis. Finally, the BTRCA technique can provide maximum value to the organization only if it makes a realistic assessment. Hence, if organizational politics are likely to bias the results, it may be preferable to rely on external consultants to conduct the analysis.

The BTRCA should examine a number of readiness and capacity factors. The most common are presented below together with examples of questions that need to be answered to identify and analyze them.

- Motivation: Do all stakeholders buy into the TEA and TP? Are all stakeholders committed to implement the TEA and execute the TP?

- Leadership and governance: Does the organization have the leadership skills to execute the TP? Are adequate governance structures in place to support the transformation of the organization? If not, can they be put in place?

- Financial capacity: Does the organization have the financial capacity to fund the execution of the TP? If not, how can this capacity be improved?

- Human resource capacity: How many human resources can the organization free up to work on the execution of the TP? Are there enough people with the right skills available? Should the organization hire more resources or rely on outside expertise?

- Partners' transformation capacity: When transformations extend beyond the boundaries of the organization and impact partners: (1) Will these partners welcome the change? (2) Will these partners have the capacity to execute their parts of the transformations? (3) Will the current contracts become roadblocks to the execution of the transformations? (4) Will these partners benefit from the transformations or will they ask for financial compensation?

- Rate of transformation: What rate of transformation is the organization capable of absorbing? Has the organization finished absorbing previous transformations?

With regard to the rate of transformation, we must emphasize that each organization has to determine its own optimal rate. If people are hit with too many transformations and are not given enough time to absorb them, they can become overwhelmed. In the words of Accenture (2013, p. 8):

Many organizations have an inherent tempo at which they can change, and [Chief Strategy Officers][7] must take care not to pursue change at a pace that may be faster than the organization can accommodate.

For more information on how to perform a BTRCA, we refer the reader to the Canadian government's Business Transformation Enablement Program (BTEP), which has defined a technique to assess an organization's readiness and capacity to change. Its documentation can be found on the Internet. Alternatively, the BTEP technique is also discussed in The Open Group Architecture Framework (TOGAF) documentation (Open Group, 2009–2011), which is also available on the Internet.

Business Transformation Risk Analysis

The intent of a Business Transformation Risk Analysis (BTRA) is to identify and mitigate risks inherent to the TP in order to minimize the number and impact of unwelcome surprises during its execution. Like the BTRCA, the BTRA should focus on risks that apply to the TP as a whole, are common to multiple projects, or need to be mitigated long before the start of some projects. However, there is an important difference between the two techniques. Whereas the identified readiness and capacity factors are guaranteed to affect projects and programs if not managed beforehand, there is only a certain likelihood that each of the identified risks will materialize.

Performing a BTRA involves the following steps:

1. Identify the risk types

    Create a list of the types of risks to be analyzed (e.g., financial, timeline, reputation, market).

2. Determine the organization's tolerance for each risk type

---

[7] The original text reads "CSOs."

For each risk type, determine the level of risk the organization is willing to tolerate (e.g., very low, low, moderate, high, critical).

3.   Identify the risks

To identify risks, all sources of risks should be scanned using techniques such as interviews, brainstorming, benchmarking and auditing. Potential sources of risks include such things as markets, regulations, leadership, incentive systems, resources, cultures, technologies, suppliers and partners. Once identified, each risk must be classified within the appropriate risk type.

4.   Score each risk

Take the following actions to score each risk. First, identify the potential impacts the risk could have if it were to materialize (e.g., cost, time, scope, quality, reputation, environment). Then, using the scale on the horizontal axis of the matrix presented in Table 4.2 (i.e., potential impacts), score these combined potential impacts. Next, using the scale on the vertical axis of the matrix presented in Table 4.2 (i.e., likelihood), score the likelihood that the risk will materialize. Finally, using the combined potential impacts and likelihood scores, and the matrix shown in Table 4.2, determine each risk's overall risk score. An overall risk score can be very low, low, moderate, high or critical.

5.   Define means of mitigating each risk

Take the following actions for each risk. First, determine if the risk is excessive by comparing its overall score to the organization's tolerance level for that type of risk. If it is excessive, use the risk tolerance level for that type of risk to define a risk mitigation goal for that specific risk. Then, define measures for mitigating this risk that reduce their impacts, likelihood, or both. The risk mitigation measures are usually simple actions, purposely designed work packages to be executed as part of the TP or changes to the TEA. After that, identify

Table 4.2: Risk score matrix

Overall risk score					
	Combined potential impacts				
Likelihood	Insignificant impacts	Minor impacts	Moderate impacts	Major impacts	Catastrophic impacts
Near certain	Moderate risk	Moderate risk	High risk	Critical risk	Critical risk
Very likely	Low risk	Moderate risk	Moderate risk	High risk	Critical risk
Likely	Low risk	Moderate risk	Moderate risk	Moderate risk	High risk
Unlikely	Very low risk	Low risk	Moderate risk	Moderate risk	Moderate risk
Negligible	Very low risk	Very low risk	Low risk	Low risk	Moderate risk

and score the residual risk (i.e., the risk that will remain once the original risk has been mitigated using the identified measures). If the residual risk is still greater than the tolerance level for that type of risk, identify further measures of mitigating it until it falls below the identified tolerance level.

While conducting the BTRA, it is also important to capture key information about each risk. This key information is shown in Table 4.3.

Business Case Analysis

Business case analysis is a popular decision-making and planning technique that qualitatively and quantitatively identifies all the anticipated pros and cons of executing a given project or program. Essentially, it provides answers, in business terms (e.g., costs, benefits, risks), to the following question: "What happens if we undertake that project/program, and what happens if we don't?"

A good business case should comprise the following key components:

•   Executive summary: A description of the business opportunity and the main transformations required to reap these benefits.

Table 4.3: Key information to capture about each risk

Information	Description
Name	Name of the risk
Potential impacts	Qualitative and quantitative description of the potential impacts the risk could have
Type	Type of risk (as per the risk type list)
Source	Does the risk originate from an internal or external source?
Inherent risk score	Risk score before the risk has been mitigated
Risk tolerance	Tolerance level for this type of risk
Risk mitigation	Planned means of mitigating the risk
Residual risk score	Potential impact level, likelihood level, and risk score after the mitigating measures have been applied

- Project/Program scope: A list and description of all the transformations included in the project/program.

- Project/Program benefits: A list of the contributions the project/program will make to the four stakeholder value propositions, and when these contributions are expected to materialize.

- Project/Program criticality: An identification of whether the project/ program is essential or optional to the implementation of the strategy, and a description of why.

- Resource requirements: A list of the resources and amount thereof that will be required, and when, to complete the project/program.

- Project/Program duration: The length of time the project/program is expected to take from start to finish.

- Project/Program assumptions: A list of the main assumptions on which the project/program is based upon.

- Project/Program constraints: A list and description of key factors constraining the project/program (e.g., completion date imposed by regulations).

- Project/Program success factors: A list of the factors that must be in place for the project/program to be able to succeed.

- Project/Program risks: A list of the risks inherent to the project/ program, together with their likelihood, potential impacts and the measures by which they can be mitigated.

- Impacts of not doing the project/program: The consequences of not executing the project/program.

Project Scoring and Ranking Analysis

Project scoring and ranking analysis is a technique used to score and rank projects according to their business benefits and risks. Although this technique is the same as the one proposed by the traditional approach to PPM, we use it to complement the result chain mapping technique, and not as the primary technique for selecting and prioritizing projects. It is needed to complement the result chain technique for two reasons. First, transformation dependencies identified in the result chain are not always sufficient to determine the optimal sequencing of projects. Indeed, the result chain technique often identifies many more essential projects that could be executed in parallel than the organization's capacity allows. The project scoring and ranking technique then becomes useful to identify which of these projects should be done first and which should be done later. Second, once the projects that are essential to the implementation of the strategy have been added to the TP, the project scoring and ranking technique can be used to identify optional projects that could be included in the TP if adequate transformation capacity remains.

The project scoring and ranking technique begins with the identification of the criteria, and their relative weights, that will be used to score each project's benefits and risks. We typically score the benefits of projects on the basis of their net contributions to each of the four stakeholder value propositions. The risk criteria used depend on the risk classification the organization uses. For example, the following risk criteria could be used to score projects: (1) customer and market risks; (2) magnitude of change risks; (3) management and execution risks; (4) partner and supplier risks; (5) technical risks; and (6) implementation risks. Next, the benefits and risks for each project are scored by assigning a score to each criterion, multiplying this score by its weight and then adding all the weighted scores (Table 4.4). The score given to each criterion is based on the information provided in the project's business case, while the guidelines on how to score against each criterion should be defined beforehand to ensure uniformity. For example, a low risk may score 1 while a moderate

Table 4.4: Scoring matrix example

Criterion	Weight	Project A	
		Score	Weighted Score
Benefit			
Contribution to the owner value proposition	35%	3	1.05
Contribution to the customer value proposition	35%	5	1.75
Contribution to the employee value proposition	15%	3	0.45
Contribution to the partner value proposition	15%	5	0.75
Total Benefit Score			**4**
Risk			
Customer and market risks	16.7%	1	0.17
Magnitude of change risks	16.7%	3	0.50
Management and execution risks	16.7%	3	0.50
Partner and supplier risks	16.7%	1	0.17
Technical risks	16.7%	1	0.17
Implementation risks	16.7%	1	0.17
Total Risk Score			**1.7**

risk may score 3 and a high risk 5. Once the value and risks of each project are scored, graphical methods such as bubble graphs (Figure 4.2) can be used to visually rank projects. If, for example, the bubble chart in Figure 4.2 was used to rank projects and the size of the bubbles represented the cost of each one, these projects would typically be ranked in order of importance by moving along the diagonal going from the top left to the bottom right.

Roadmapping

The purpose of roadmapping is to sequence on a timeline when each transformation project is planned to be executed. This sequencing is based on the dependencies that exist between the projects, the transformation risks, the ranking of each project, and the extended organization's readiness and capacity to transform itself. The result is a roadmap diagram similar to a project management Gantt chart (Figure 4.9). The critical path of the TP is defined as the project sequence that determines the shortest time required to execute the complete TP (shown in gray in Figure 4.9).

Transformation Plan Optimization

The transformation plan optimization technique entails two steps. During the first step, which should be conducted after creating a first draft of the TP using the techniques described above, the TP team identifies issues affecting this draft plan. These issues can be of several types. For example:

1. The feasibility of completely transforming a given capability in a single project may be low because the costs, risks or time required is too great;

2. Too many transformations may be bundled in the same project, making it unacceptably large and risky;

3. At certain times, the TP may either require more transformation capacity than is available or may underutilize available capacity;

4. The delays between the times when the transformation costs are incurred and their benefits materialize may be too long;

5. The TP's critical path may be judged to be too long;

6. The TP may schedule the transformation of some capabilities too rapidly relative to the transformation of other related capabilities; and

7. During the execution of the TP, the customer value proposition (CVP) may temporarily become confusing for customers. That is, while the TP is being executed, the transitional CVP may comprise elements from both the old and the target CVP that give customers conflicting messages and create a mismatch between the transitional CVP and customers' expectations. This kind of mismatch has been the downfall of many organizations.

During the second step, the TP team determines how the identified issues may be resolved. To do so, one or more of the following approaches can be used:

1. Breaking large projects down into series of smaller projects;

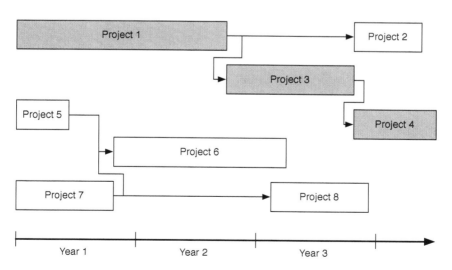

Figure 4.9: Sample roadmap (critical path shown in gray)

2. Temporarily substituting lengthy prerequisite transformations, which significantly delay the start of essential transformations, by quick interim transformations. Indeed, it may be possible to enable the early transformation of several building blocks by making minimal temporary transformations to the building blocks upon which they depend instead of waiting for them to be fully transformed. The building blocks that were temporarily transformed can be fully transformed later on. However, care should be taken not to add too many temporary transformations as they increase the costs and efforts required to execute the TP as a whole.

3. Making changes to the TEA. This should only be done when the issues with the TP are important and no other means of resolving them can be found.

4. Shifting projects in time.

The Methodology

Before we describe our target-architecture-based methodology, we must make three recommendations as to how it should be implemented and used. First, the methodology should be implemented incrementally. This methodology is fairly complex and attempting to implement it all at once, without a strong planning culture, can be a significant challenge. The way in which it should be implemented and thus the sequence in which the techniques should be adopted depends on the organization's current planning methodology. Second, the process of elaborating the TP should be iterative, as it should be executed every time the architecture of a new slice of the TBA is completed. Each of these iteration should account for all of the slices of the organization architected to date. Third, although the TP generally covers a three- to five-year time span, we recommend that only the first two or three years of the TP be detailed while the remaining years should only be outlined. This approach is most efficient because it is very likely that changes will occur during the coming years (e.g., unforeseen events that impact the organization's transformation projects, financial situation, and external environment) that will require parts of the TP to be modified, perhaps significantly. In addition, developing a full TP would require a significant amount of time and effort and would needlessly delay the start of its execution. After year one of the TP is complete, the first of the upcoming years that had only been outlined should be detailed and the plan should be extended with the outline of one more year, and so on until the organizational transformation is complete and the organization is able to execute its strategy in full (if ever).

Our 10-phase target-architecture-based methodology is anchored in the techniques described above and is depicted in Figure 4.10. The first phase, Initiation (P_1), comprises four activities. During the first activity, Create Transformation Plan Team (P_1A_1), the TP team members are identified. This team should include business architects, IT enterprise architects, subject matter experts (SMEs) from each business area that will be impacted by the transformations included in the TP, one or more senior project managers, and possibly other professionals depending on the nature of the transformations to be made. The TP team should also include an accountant, whose responsibility is to ensure that the financial analyses included in the business cases are done properly (i.e., comply with recognized accounting practices). Since a good understanding of the transformations to be executed is key to the elaboration of the TP, business architects should assume prime responsibility for building the TP but should work closely with the other team members. The project managers on the team should be responsible for coordinating the evaluation of project costs and efforts and act as advisors to the business architects with respect to risk identification and mitigation, and readiness and capacity issues. In the second activity, Create the TP Elaboration Plan (P_1A_2), the project plan for the elaboration of the TP is defined. The third activity, Define Project Scoring Criteria (P_1A_3), is when the scoring and ranking criteria to be used to compare projects are defined and approved by the Transformation Governance Board (TGB). The role of the TGB is

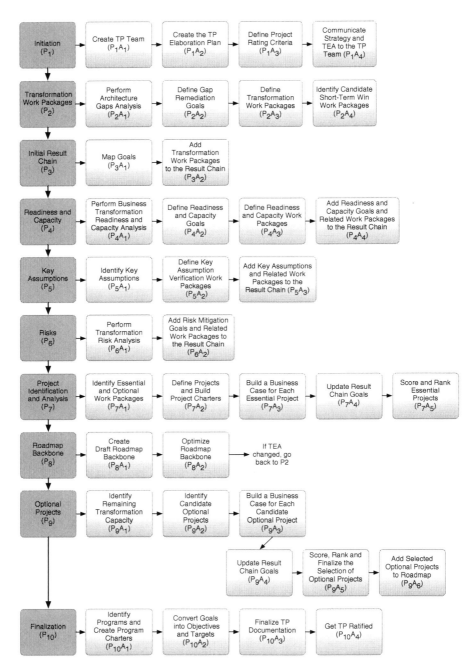

Figure 4.10: Target-architecture-based methodology

described in detail in Chapter 6. Finally, in the fourth activity, Communicate Strategy and TEA to the TP Team (P_1A_4), the strategy and TEA are communicated to the members of the TP team to ensure understanding and get buy-in.

The second phase, Transformation Work Packages (P_2), also comprises four activities. During the first, Perform Architecture Gaps Analysis (P_2A_1), the gaps between the current and target states of each enterprise architecture building block are identified. In the second activity, Define Gap Remediation Goals (P_2A_2), each architecture gap is translated into a gap remediation goal (e.g., Process A automated; Information system B deployed; Technology Z developed). During the third activity, Define Transformation Work Packages (P_2A_3), the work packages required to fill each gap (i.e., reach each gap remediation goal) are defined. And in the fourth activity, Identify Candidate Short-Term Win Work Packages (P_2A_4), short-term win work packages, which can be executed rapidly, provide significant gains and build the organization's confidence in its ability to transform itself, are chosen from amongst all the work packages defined in P_2A_3.

The Initial Result Chain phase (P_3) comprises two activities. During the first activity, Map Goals (P_3A_1), the construction of the TP's result chain is started with the mapping, as shown in Figure 4.11, of the gap remediation goals defined in P_2A_2 and all the other transformation goals defined while formulating the strategy and architecting the TEA (i.e., performance improvement and stakeholder value proposition goals). During the second activity, Add Transformation Work Packages to the Result Chain (P_3A_2), transformation work packages are added to the result chain and linked to both the goals that must be achieved before they are executed and the goals they will contribute to, as shown in Figure 4.12.

The Readiness and Capacity phase (P_4) comprises four activities. During the first one, Perform Business Transformation Readiness and Capacity Analysis (P_4A_1), the readiness and capacity gaps that need to be

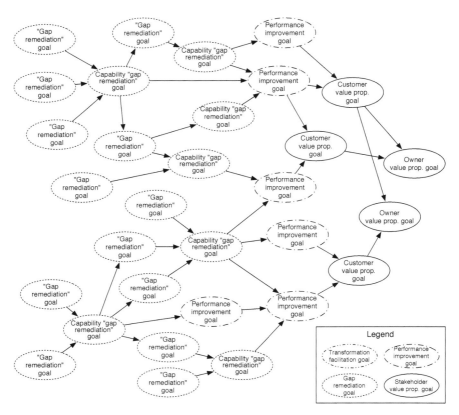

Figure 4.11: Result chain with gap remediation, performance improvement and stakeholder value proposition goals (P₃A₁)

remediated to successfully execute the planned transformation work packages are identified and analyzed. During the second, Define Readiness and Capacity Goals (P₄A₂), each readiness and capacity gap is translated into a transformation facilitation goal (e.g., Have a team of 10 Lean Six Sigma black belts). In the third activity, Define Readiness and Capacity Work Packages (P₄A₃), the work packages required to reach each of the readiness or capacity goals are defined. Finally, during the fourth activity, Add Readiness and Capacity Goals and Related Work Packages to the Result Chain (P_4A_4), the readiness and capacity goals and their related work packages are added to the result chain, as shown in Figure 4.12.

The fifth phase, Key Assumptions (P_5), comprises three activities. During the first activity, Identify Key Assumptions (P_5A_1), the key assumptions related to the strategy, TEA and TP that represent necessary conditions for the execution of the strategy but over which the organization has little or no control are identified. During the second activity, Define Key Assumption Verification Work Packages (P_5A_2), the work packages that will need to be executed during the execution of the TP to validate (or invalidate) the key assumptions are defined. These work packages are typically of the following types: analyses, pilot projects and transformation results tracking. In the third activity, Add Key Assumptions and Related Work Packages to the Result Chain (P_5A_3), the key assumptions and the work packages required to validate them are added to the result chain, as shown in Figure 4.12.

The Risks phase (P_6) comprises two activities. During the first, Perform Transformation Risk Analysis (P_6A_1), the transformation risks are identified and scored, and risk mitigation goals and work packages are defined. During the second activity, Add Risk Mitigation Goals and Related Work Packages to the Result Chain (P_6A_2), the risk mitigation goals and related work packages are added to the result chain, as shown in Figure 4.12.

The Project Identification and Analysis phase (P_7) has five activities. During the first, Identify Essential and Optional Work Packages (P_7A_1), all of the work packages defined so far (i.e., transformation, readiness and capacity, risk, and assumption work packages) are identified as being either essential or optional to the implementation of the strategy. Note that a transformation work package should be identified as essential when it is a prerequisite to another transformation work package previously identified as essential, while readiness and capacity, risk mitigation, and assumption work packages are deemed essential when they enable essential transformation work packages. During the second activity, Define

Projects and Build Project Charters (P_7A_2), the work packages are grouped into projects designed to deliver coherent, operative results (Figure 4.12), and the charter for each project is documented. Because essential work packages constitute the backbone of the TP, it is preferable for each project to comprise either essential or optional transformation work packages but not both. This is done to avoid overburdening essential projects, which would reduce their benefits, delay their delivery and increase their risks, as well as create capacity issues and make it difficult to optimize the TP. The short-term win work packages identified in P_2A_4 for which significant risk, readiness or transformation capacity issues have later been identified should be reclassified as normal work packages and grouped into regular essential or optional projects. The remaining short-term win work packages should form the core of independent essential projects and should be grouped with as few other work packages as possible in order to avoid overburdening these projects and reducing the feasibility of executing them quickly. Once all projects have been defined, the charter of each essential and optional project should be written. During the third activity, Build a Business Case for Each Essential Project (P_7A_3), a business case is prepared for each essential project. Amongst other things, these business cases serve to better quantify the goals that are attainable by each project (i.e., what benefits each project can realistically generate). In the fourth activity, Update Result Chain Goals (P_7A_4), the goals in the result chain that relate to essential projects are updated to reflect the benefits estimated in their business cases. And during the fifth, Score and Rank Essential Projects (P_7A_5), the essential projects are scored and ranked.

The eighth phase, Roadmap Backbone (P_8), comprises two activities. During the first activity, Create Draft Roadmap Backbone (P_8A_1), taking into account the dependencies identified in the result chain, the scores of the essential projects and the remaining short-term win projects, a first draft of the roadmap that sequences only the essential projects is created. During the second activity, Optimize Roadmap Backbone (P_8A_2), issues affecting the

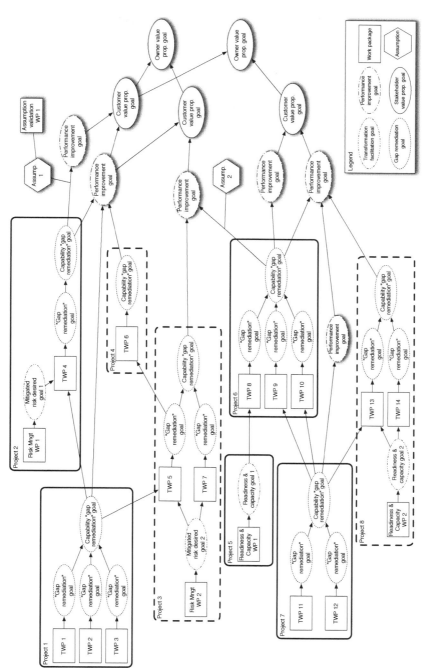

Figure 4.12: Project identification (P_7A_2)

roadmap backbone are identified and resolved. It is important to note here that this optimization may occasionally require that changes be made to the TEA. When that is the case, phases 2 to 7 need to be revisited.

The Optional Projects phase (P_9) comprises six activities. During the first, Identify Remaining Transformation Capacity (P_9A_1), any remaining transformation capacity is identified. If such capacity does exist, then during the second activity, Identify Candidate Optional Projects (P_9A_2), the candidate optional projects identified in P_7A_2 that could be included in the TP are identified. This should be done while taking into consideration the nature and timing of the available transformation capacity together with the dependencies identified in the result chain, the readiness of the extended organization to transform itself, and the risks of the optional projects. During the third activity, Build a Business Case for Each Candidate Optional Project (P_9A_3), a business case is prepared for each optional project. During the fourth activity, Update Result Chain Goals (P_9A_4), goals in the result chain that relate to optional projects are updated, just as those that relate to essential projects were updated during activity P_7A_4. In the fifth activity, Score, Rank and Finalize the Selection of Optional Projects (P_9A_5), each candidate optional project is scored and ranked and the best projects are selected. During the sixth activity, Add Selected Optional Projects to Roadmap (P_9A_6), the selected optional projects are added to the roadmap. At the end of this activity, an estimated completion date for each project included in the roadmap is set.

The tenth and last phase, Finalization (P_{10}), comprises four activities. During the first one, Identify Programs and Create Program Charters ($P_{10}A_1$), projects that need to be coordinated together to make it possible to attain goals that would be difficult to achieve otherwise are grouped into programs and a charter is created for each of these programs. During the second activity, Convert Goals into Objectives and Targets ($P_{10}A_2$), the project business cases and the roadmap are used to quantify the goals in the result chain and estimate when each one will be attained in whole or in part. By doing so, the goals in the result chain are converted into objectives and targets. In the third activity, Finalize TP Documentation ($P_{10}A_3$), all of the documentation for the TP is completed. This activity also includes the creation of an executive summary which includes a list, a high-level description of each of the projects included in the TP, the roadmap showing when the projects are planned to be executed, their respective anticipated benefits, and the resources required to complete each project. The executive summary should also include a summarized result chain showing only projects and programs, not work packages, to facilitate communication and executive-level discussions about the TP. A work-package-level result chain is an important working document for the TP team, but not for executives. During the fourth activity, Get TP Ratified ($P_{10}A_4$), the TP is ratified by the TGB.

4.6. The Concept Map

To complete our discussion of the elaboration of the TP, Figure 4.13 presents the relationships that exist between the various concepts at the heart of a sound TP. This concept map can be summarized as follows. Architecture gaps exist between the building blocks of the CEA and TEA. Work packages are defined to achieve goals, some of which are to wholly or partly remediate one or more architecture gaps. Some work packages are feasible only if dependent work packages achieve their own goals. Work packages are grouped into projects, which can be grouped into programs. The transformation plan sequences the execution of the projects. Finally, business cases are used to score and rank projects; a business case comprises a project's goals, costs, efforts and risks.

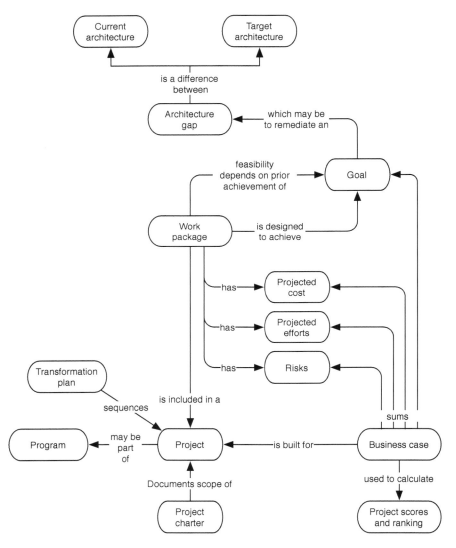

Figure 4.13: Map of transformation plan concepts

References

Accenture (2013) *The Agility-Creating Chief Strategy Officer: Bringing Speed to Change.*

Fujitsu Consulting, and Thorp, J. (1998). *The Information Paradox: Realizing the Business Benefits of Information Technology.* Fujitsu Consulting, Canada.

Project Management Institute (2008) *The Standard for Project Portfolio Management,* Second Edition. Project Management Institute.

Open Group (2009–2011) *The Open Group Standard: TOGAF Version 9.1.* The Open Group.

Zagotta, R., and Robinson, D. (2002) Keys to Successful Strategy Execution. *Journal of Business Strategy,* 23(1), 30-34.

Chapter 5

Engaging and Governing

Business architects should also play an active support role in the Engage and Govern group of activities that successful organizations rely upon to formulate, implement and execute their strategy. As described in Chapter 1, the engage activities are concerned with motivating and getting buy-in from all stakeholders and with removing barriers. The govern activities, in turn, involve monitoring events, learning from new information and insights, and making necessary adjustments to the strategic plan and its execution. The objective of this chapter is to describe the engage and govern activities that are relevant to business architects' work and to explain the contributions business architects can make to each of these activities. This chapter has two sections focusing on engage activities and govern activities, respectively.

Before we begin, it is important to mention that most of the engage and govern activities described in this chapter correspond to best practices previously described by leading authors such as Kaplan and Norton (1996, 2005, 2008), Kotter (1996), Kotter and Cohen (2002), Coon and Wolf (2005), McChesney, Covey and Huling (2012), Mankins and Steele (2005), Zagotta and Robinson (2002), Martin (2010), Myers (2001) and Sull (2007).

Engage

As we mentioned above, the engage activities are concerned with motivating and getting buy-in from all stakeholders, and with removing barriers to the formulation, implementation and execution of the strategy. Five of these activities are relevant to the work of business architects: (1) establish and maintain a sense of urgency; (2) build and expand the guiding coalition; (3) communicate the strategic plan and the progress of its execution; (4) cascade objectives and tie incentives to their achievement; and (5) implement agile financial processes that are well integrated into the organization's other planning processes. Some of these activities correspond to key steps in the eight-stage process for creating change proposed by Kotter (1996). The following subsections describe these five activities.

Establish and Maintain a Sense of Urgency

To successfully formulate, implement and execute its strategy, an organization must establish a sense of urgency in order to break down people's natural resistance to change (Kotter, 1996) and trigger the process of formulating a new or revised strategy. This sense of urgency must also be maintained throughout the implementation and execution of the selected strategy. To establish and maintain this sense of urgency, the organization must remove or minimize the impacts of sources of complacency. This can be done in a variety of ways including taking bold and even risky actions when necessary (e.g., creating a crisis by allowing a financial loss to occur so that key members of the organization become aware of the company's weaknesses), using external experts to gather relevant data and foster honest discussions about the situation (Kotter, 1996), and repeatedly communicating to all stakeholders the challenges the organization is currently facing or is expecting to face. In addition, the organization must give the required autonomy to the middle and lower-level managers who are instrumental in creating the conditions that are essential for implementing and executing the strategy.

Business architects should contribute to the establishment and maintenance of a sense of urgency by communicating to stakeholders at all levels of the organization about the new best practices other organizations are already successfully using as well as the issues and insights they have discovered while analyzing how their organization works. To be most effective in establishing and maintaining this sense of urgency, business architects should communicate their messages using facts and other tools, such as customer anecdotes, to reach people at both the logical and emotional levels.

Build and Expand the Guiding Coalition

Successfully transforming an organization is 70% to 90% leadership and only 10% to 30% management (Kotter, 1996). Hence, a strong, credible, and trustworthy guiding coalition that acts as a team with a common goal must be created at the onset of formulating, implementing and executing the strategy and must be given the proper authority to successfully lead the change. The guiding coalition must be made up of members with positions of power, broad expertise, strong credibility and proven leadership skills (Kotter, 1996), who are committed to seeing the transformation of the organization through. During the formulation of the strategy, the guiding coalition should include executives and a handful of strategists, business architects and subject matter experts (SMEs), all of whom can contribute to the strategy formulation in their own way. During the design of the target business architecture (TBA) and corresponding target technology architectures (TTAs), the guiding coalition should be expanded to include additional leaders and SMEs. It should be further expanded during the elaboration of the transformation plan (TP) to include program managers and accountants. It should then be expanded even further during the execution of the TP to include additional managers and SMEs who will be involved in the execution of the projects and programs included in the TP. The addition of these new members is essential to cope with the countless decisions that must be made during the execution of the TP and to do all the convincing that will be required to implement these decisions. Although most members of the guiding coalition should be employees of the organization, it can be very beneficial to include external experts.

Business architects are key players in the guiding coalition. Indeed, because of their expertise and referent power, and because of the central role they play in architecting the TBA and elaborating the TP, it is crucial for them to participate in the guiding coalition.

Communicate the Strategic Plan and the Progress of Its Execution

To successfully lead the formulation, implementation and execution of the strategy, the guiding coalition must continuously invest a substantial amount of time and effort in communicating the strategic plan and the progress of its execution to all stakeholders. Indeed, the real power of a transformational vision can only be unleashed when the people involved in its implementation understand it well and buy into it (Kotter, 1996). To succeed in the challenging intellectual and emotional task of getting a critical mass of people from the "Why do we need to do this? Everything is just fine as it is" mindset to a "We have to do this" mindset and keeping them there, communication of the strategic plan and the progress of its execution must follow six key guidelines.

1.   The messages must clearly explain the strategic plan and why the strategy must be implemented to all stakeholders to get their buy-in and to let them know what they must do to contribute to the

implementation of the transformational vision (Kotter, 1996; Kotter and Cohen, 2002).

2. Communication must be two-way (Coon and Wolf, 2005; Kotter, 1996). By answering questions and gathering comments from the various stakeholders, the guiding coalition can identify the intellectual and emotional concerns preventing stakeholders from buying into the strategic plan, and then address these concerns. Open two-way communication throughout the formulation, implementation and execution of the strategy also allows executives, strategists, business architects and other stakeholders to gather important insights that may have been missed previously and, as a result, to make any necessary adjustments to the strategic plan and its execution. Indeed, the literature on strategy abounds with accounts of people at all levels of the organization who had important information and insights that, once considered, led to important improvements in the formulation, implementation, and/or execution of their organization's strategy. A famous example of this is Honda's success in penetrating the motorcycle market in North America during the 1960s. The new insights gathered by the team that had been newly deployed in America enabled Honda to change its initial strategy, the initial reception of which was lukewarm, into one that rapidly became a resounding success (Mintzberg et al., 1996).

3. Because people in the organization change, new questions arise, and people's motivation can easily dwindle, the issues the organization faces, the strategic plan and the status of its execution should be communicated frequently. One message per year is just not enough for people to keep a high sense of motivation (Kotter, 1996).

4. Leaders at all levels of the organization should play an active role in communicating the strategic plan and the status of its execution so people throughout the organization can feel that their leaders are committed to the implementation and execution of the strategy.

5. The communication must be tailored to the various groups within the organization to maximize buy-in and enable people to fully understand how they are personally expected to contribute or will be otherwise impacted by the formulation, implementation and execution of the strategy. It is important to note, however, that the strategic plan should not always be communicated in full to all members of the organization, particularly in cases where important strategic information could be leaked to competitors or when it could scare or demotivate certain employees.

6. Communication must reveal the progress made in achieving strategic objectives in order to help establish and maintain a feeling of "We can do this" (Kaplan and Norton, 1996; Kotter, 1996; Kotter and Cohen, 2002; McChesney, Covey and Huling, 2012).

Business architects can contribute to the communication of the strategic plan and the progress of its execution in two complementary ways. They can help prepare material that explains what transformations must be executed to implement the strategy, and why. In addition, they can help executives and other leaders in their communication efforts by preparing answers to questions people may have about the strategic plan and the implementation of the strategy.

Cascade Targets and Tie Incentives to Their Achievement

To succeed in formulating, implementing and executing its strategy, an organization should cascade the targets of the strategic plan into personal targets down the entire organizational structure and, if it has an incentive program, tie incentives to the achievement of these targets. Indeed, this cascade process, which translates the transformation targets defined in the strategic plan into personal targets, not only clarifies what each person is responsible for with respect to the formulation, implementation and execution of the strategic plan but also makes each and every person involved accountable for meeting these personal targets.

The process of cascading targets and tying incentives to their achievement comprises two major steps. First, targets should be cascaded in a top-down fashion throughout the organizational structure. The cascade should start with the assignment of personal targets to each CXO under the CEO. These should then be translated into personal targets for the CXOs' direct reports and so on until targets have been assigned to all members of the organization. Second, incentives should be tied to the achievement of these personal targets.

It is important to mention here that the targets set by an organization must be realistic. Indeed, it is unlikely that the formulation, implementation and execution of the strategy will be successful if there is not a critical mass of people within the organization who are confident that they can achieve their own targets and, as a team, achieve the organization's targets. As a matter of fact, we have learned from personal experience that setting unrealistic targets can destroy people's motivation.

Because they have been heavily involved in architecting the TBA, the elaboration of the TP and the identification of the transformation goals, objectives and targets, business architects are in a unique position to support the process of breaking down objectives into targets and cascading these targets down the entire organizational structure.

Implement Agile Financial Processes That Are Well Integrated into the Organization's Other Planning Processes

Most organizations face two important issues in their budgeting and long-term financial planning processes that significantly hinder the formulation, implementation and execution of their strategy (Hunt, 2006; Kaplan and Norton, 2005; Mankins and Steele, 2005; Myers, 2001). The first issue is that the budgeting process generally lacks the agility needed for organizations to be able to optimize the use of their transformation capacity and smoothly implement their strategy. The yearly process of getting funding for projects typically goes as follows. The process starts with a four- to six-month budget preparation period. During that time, managers propose projects that will improve their org unit's performance. These project proposals then percolate through the management hierarchy and those that remain at the end are slated for execution during the coming financial year. Once the new budgets are available, the next few months are spent assembling the project teams, planning the execution of these projects, and negotiating contracts with suppliers for required resources. Once the projects are initiated, the teams rush to get them done before their funding dries up at the end of the financial year. The result is a six- to nine-month period during which a burst of transformations is executed followed by a period of several months during which fewer transformations are executed and managers focus on preparing business cases to support their project proposals for the following year. This process wastes resources and is difficult to adapt once the transformation projects start. Indeed, if midway through the financial year the organization needs to stop some projects in order to reduce expenditures, all the efforts and expenditures made in these projects so far will have been wasted and the expenditures will have to be transferred from capital investments to operating expenses. If, on the contrary, the financial situation is better than expected and would enable the organization to launch additional transformation projects, it is very difficult to capture these opportunities, and thus accelerate the execution of the TP, because no manager is willing to go through the process of resetting financial assumptions and reviewing business cases for the second time in the year to decide which additional projects should be initiated.

The yearly budget process also wastes resources because projects that cannot be completed as planned during the financial year must have parts of their budget carried over to the next financial year. These carryovers represent currently available transformation capacity that will not be used. To make matters worse, it is not easy to identify and use this unused capacity to start other projects because project managers are cautious and wait until the last possible moment to disclose how much of their budget will have to be carried over to the next financial year.

The second issue most organizations face with respect to their budgeting and long-term financial planning is that these processes are not well integrated with each other and with the organization's other planning processes. Indeed, when organizations create their budgets and long-term financial plans, they generally fail to correctly account for the size and timing of the revenues, expenses and cash flows that are likely to occur as a result of the implementation and execution of the strategy. Consequently, they often over-predict both the short-term and long-term financial performance gains that will be generated by executing their strategy. Under these circumstances, the owners and members of the organization are often disappointed by their organization's performance and lose confidence in its capacity to achieve its strategic objectives (Mankins and Steele, 2005).

To cope with the inability of yearly budgets to keep pace with today's dynamic business environments, organizations should make two important changes. The first is to move from a yearly budget process to a rolling financial forecast process. Every month or quarter, the organization should revise its financial assumptions (e.g., revenues, costs, investments and cash flow forecasts) and build a new financial forecast for the next 12 to 18 months (Hope and Fraser, 2003; Hunt, 2006; Myers, 2001), adding a new month or quarter at the end of the forecast each time. This kind of continuous approach provides executives with a much more accurate and timely picture of how much money can be allocated to strategic initiatives, which in turn allows them to be much more responsive to changing financial situations. If the situation improves, they can, at any point in time, increase the pace at which they initiate new projects. If, on the contrary, things go worse, they can reduce expenditures by slowing the pace at which they start new projects, possibly down to zero, instead of stopping ongoing projects and wasting the investments made in them so far.

Many people object to the use of a rolling financial forecast, thinking that the effort required to produce each new forecast is comparable to that required to prepare a yearly budget. On the contrary, a rolling financial forecast requires much less effort since the underlying financial assumptions generally change only slightly from one forecast to the next – far less than those for two consecutive yearly budgets. Having a TP on hand can further reduce these efforts. Indeed, by elaborating the TP beforehand, all of the work required to decide which projects should be funded next will already have been done and all the necessary financial information about these projects will already be available in their business cases.

The second change organizations should make to add agility to their transformation process is to centralize their transformation budget at the business unit or parent organization level, depending on the operating model chosen, instead of distributing it to executives and managers at the start of the financial year. Centralizing the transformation budget enables organizations to allocate financial resources to projects as needed and not to have to hound managers to find funds to transfer to other projects when additional money is needed. It also helps to get rid of the "This is my budget, I'll spend it the way I want" mentality that exists in many organizations and makes it difficult to ensure that the projects that are executed are aligned with the strategy.

Finally, organizations should align their rolling financial forecasts and long-term financial plans with the TP. An organization should make sure that the revenues, expenditures, investments and related financial benefits planned in the rolling financial forecasts and long-term financial plan agree in timing and size with those included in the TP.

Business architects can help the people developing the rolling financial forecasts and long-term financial plan by providing and explaining to them the information that was generated while elaborating the TP (e.g., costs, benefits and timing of each of the selected transformation projects).

Govern

As mentioned in the introduction to this chapter, govern activities are concerned with monitoring events, learning from new information and insights, and making the necessary adjustments to the strategic plan and its execution. These monitoring, learning and adapting activities form a vital feedback loop that enables the organization to successfully manage three important sources of uncertainty that exist in the formulation, implementation and execution of its strategy: (1) the unavoidably incomplete and imperfect information the organization must rely on while initially formulating its strategy; (2) the numerous issues that transformation projects inevitably encounter (e.g., time delays, unexpected costs, supplier issues, and difficulties executing certain transformations); and (3) the unpredictable nature of the organization's external environment (e.g., moves made by competitors, suppliers and complementors, new opportunities, potential shifts in customer demand, new technologies, and new regulations).

To be effective, however, these monitoring, learning and adapting activities must be conducted at three different levels: (1) the individual projects or programs; (2) the TEA and TP; and (3) the strategy. This section describes the governance activities that should be conducted at each of these levels during the formulation, implementation and execution of the strategy and that are relevant to the work of business architects.

Before we describe these activities, it is important to highlight three success factors that the govern activities at all three levels share. First, executives and other leaders must absolutely participate in these activities. Their involvement sends a clear message across the organization that the formulation, implementation and execution of the strategy is very important. It also allows executives to become rapidly aware of new issues, events and insights, and to make any necessary adjustments to the strategy, TEA, TP and individual projects. The participation of executives and other leaders is also essential to facilitate coordination across the numerous transformation-related and non-transformation-related initiatives (e.g., product development, major maintenance projects) taking place throughout the organization.

Second, the govern activities at all three levels should be structured around a series of regularly scheduled meetings dedicated to reviewing progress, results and external environmental changes, as well as analyzing issues, making sense of them, identifying possible improvement opportunities, making decisions, committing to these decisions and holding each other accountable for them. These meetings force executives and other leaders to directly experience the details of the formulation, implementation and execution of the strategy and to learn how the organization is performing (Mankins and Steele, 2005). Hence, although executives and other leaders are under pressure from their day-to-day activities and must spend a significant amount of time preparing for these meetings, their participation is critical to ensure success. Consequently, more and more organizations are making executive participation in these meetings mandatory (Accenture, 2013).

Third, the purpose of the govern activities at all three levels should not be to force people to implement and execute the strategy, implement the TEA and execute the TP exactly as originally devised but rather to help them take account of and surmount the difficulties they face while formulating, implementing and executing the strategy by leveraging the new information, insights and opportunities they discover along the way. This help can take many forms such as allocating additional resources, carrying out additional change management or leadership activities to ensure buy-in, adapting certain transformations, modifying the TP, and in some cases even changing the TEA or the strategy.

Govern Individual Projects

To successfully govern individual projects, the organization must regularly monitor their progress from three complementary perspectives: (1) transformation; (2) change management; and (3) project management. From the transformation perspective, the organization must monitor the alignment of the transformations being executed with the TEA, remain alert to new insights into these transformations, and check whether projects are achieving their objectives. From the change management perspective, the organization must monitor stakeholders' sense of urgency, buy-in and motivation to execute the desired transformations. From the project management perspective, the organization must monitor project timelines, costs, resource consumption, assumptions, and risks, as well as the extended organization's readiness and capacity to execute the projects.

The analyses of the information gathered may highlight issues that, if not addressed, will prevent the transformation projects from fully reaching their objectives. When that is the case, further analysis may be needed to identify the root causes of these issues and come up with corrective actions. As a first example, monitoring a project from a transformation perspective may reveal that the project is deviating from the TEA (i.e., some transformations are not aligned to the TEA). When that happens, the reasons for the deviation must be identified and analyzed by the project team in collaboration with the relevant enterprise architects (i.e., business architects, IT enterprise architects and/or engineers in charge of the other TTAs). If this deviation is justified, then the TEA should be updated. If the deviation is not justified, may prevent the project from reaching its objectives or may have negative impacts elsewhere in the organization, then the project should be realigned to the TEA. As a second example, monitoring a project from a change management perspective may show that the recently executed transformations are providing less than the expected benefits because many of the people impacted by these transformations were inadequately trained, did not understand why the transformations were needed or are trying to revert to their old ways of doing things. When that is the case, better training may be called for, together with additional open discussions, to ensure that all project stakeholders understand the reasons for these transformations.

As a third example, monitoring a project from the project management perspective may show that it is falling behind schedule. In that case, the project schedule should be revisited and, if necessary, more resources may be allocated to the project.

To effectively govern individual projects, the following best practices should be adopted. First, projects should be funded using a stage-gate approach with a set of three or four predefined milestones (i.e., gates) where each project is systematically reviewed before it is funded to progress to the next gate (i.e., before the next stage is funded). This approach has proven to help organizations better control project execution and correct problems before significant amounts of resources have been wasted. Second, each project should have a steering committee to oversee its progress between gates. Third, formal architecture reviews should be conducted at the gates to monitor the quality of the transformations and their alignment with the TEA, and, if need be, to help resolve architecture issues and make decisions about proposed changes. These architecture reviews should be orchestrated by the organization's Architecture Review Board (ARB) whose role is described in detail in Chapter 6. Fourth, the organization should rely on another committee, the Transformation Project Management Board (TPMB), to review and approve change requests tied to project timelines and budgets. The TPMB's role is also described in detail in Chapter 6.

Business architects can contribute to the govern activities at the level of individual projects in two ways. First, by participating in and possibly managing architecture reviews, they can help resolve business architecture issues. Second, by participating in project steering committees, they can help provide guidance to the projects.

Govern the Target Enterprise Architecture and the Transformation Plan

To successfully govern the implementation of its TEA and the execution of its TP, an organization should leverage the monitoring done at the level of individual projects to identify issues that may impact multiple projects and whose resolution may require adjustments to the TEA and/or TP. For example, leveraging change management monitoring may enable the organization to uncover shortcomings in the TEA or TP. Stakeholders may resist change because they have important insights that have not been considered, or not properly considered, during the creation of the TEA and TP, and that make them think that certain transformations will not provide the desired benefits or may even have negative impacts. When strong resistance to change is detected, it is very important to identify its root causes so possible issues in the TEA and the TP can be identified and resolved.

In addition to leveraging the govern activities conducted at the level of individual projects, the govern activities conducted at the TEA and TP level require the adoption of another practice. To serve as a focal point for these activities, the organization should create a Transformation Governance Board (TGB), which owns the TEA and TP. The TGB's role is described in detail in Chapter 6.

Business architects can contribute to the govern activities at the TEA and TP levels in two ways. First, by taking part in the formal project management and architecture reviews and establishing and maintaining close collaboration with the project teams' IT enterprise architects and other professionals, they can detect enterprise architecture issues common to multiple projects, such as misfits between different transformations, and help identify solutions for these issues in a timely manner. For example, business architects can help analyze the impacts of project timeline and cost issues on the overall TP and help find solutions to mitigate them. Second, they can report these issues to the TGB and present the solutions they recommend for resolving them.

Govern the Strategy

To successfully govern its strategy and the execution thereof, the organization must monitor internal and external events, derive new insights and identify new opportunities and threats from the information gathered, and then assess the strengths and weaknesses of the strategy and of its execution to identify necessary adjustments. External events that must be monitored include those that relate to the political, legal, economic, social, technological, ecological and climatic, and infrastructure environments together with those that relate to industry structure forces (i.e., customers, suppliers, competitors (new and old), new entrants, substitutes, and complementary products). Internally, the organization must monitor issues, new insights and realized benefits arising from the execution of the strategy.

When adjustments are required, the actions taken to adapt the strategy depend on the nature of the issues identified. For example, a competitor's move may force the organization to revise its strategy by making changes to its product and service development plan, while new market insights may lead to changes in the customer segments and geographic areas targeted.

In addition to leveraging the govern activities conducted at the individual project, TEA and TP levels, the govern activities at the level of the strategy require the adoption of a number of other best practices. First, the organization should use a scorecard to assess both its success in executing its strategy and the success of the strategy itself. Kaplan and Norton (1996), amongst others, have written extensively on this subject. The principle underlying the use of a scorecard is, as Zagotta and Robinson (2002, p. 33) put it, that *"What gets measured is what gets done, and if reporting and strategy aren't rapidly integrated, the execution is likely to flounder."* The scorecard is usually published once a month although some organizations update it as often as every week. For reasons of effectiveness, the scorecard should be accompanied by a review of recent important external events and should be used by leaders and other stakeholders to assess the progress made so far, make sense of events, hold each other accountable for meeting strategic objectives and, if need be, adapt the strategy. Although the "Balanced scorecard" introduced by Kaplan and Norton (1996) has proven to be an effective organizational performance measurement framework, we prefer to use a scorecard based on the Capability-Based Strategy Map introduced in Chapter 2. Because it includes a perspective for each of the four stakeholder value propositions and for each of the nine types of enterprise architecture building blocks, we consider that our Capability-Based Strategy Map is more complete. In addition, the organization should use activity-based profitability reports summarizing the profit-and-loss data by region, market segment, product line and customer to monitor profitability (Kaplan and Norton, 2008). Finally, to serve as a focal point for the govern activities at the strategy level, the organization should create a Strategy Governance Board (SGB) that owns the strategy on behalf of the owners of the organization. The SGB's role is described in detail in Chapter 6.

Just like they can contribute to the formulation of the strategy, business architects can contribute to the govern activities at the strategy level by providing insights and helping to analyze candidate strategy improvements and by outlining the associated TEA and TP.

References

Accenture. (2013) *The Agility-Creating Chief Strategy Officer: Bringing Speed to Change.*

Coon, B., and Wolf, S. (2005) The Alchemy of Strategy Execution. *Employment Relations Today*, 32(3), 19-30.

Hope, J., and Fraser, R. (2003) *Beyond Budgeting – How Managers Can Break Free from the Annual Performance Trap.* Harvard Business Publishing, Boston.

Hunt, S. (2006) *Building Finance and Performance Management Mastery with Superior Budgeting and Forecasting Capabilities.* Accenture.

Kaplan, R.S., and Norton, D.P. (1996) *The Balanced Scorecard: Translating Strategy into Action.* Harvard Business Publishing, Boston.

Kaplan, R.S., and Norton, D.P. (2005) The Office of Strategy Management. *Harvard Business Review*, 83(10), 72-80.

Kaplan, R.S., and Norton, D.P. (2008) *The Execution Premium: Linking Strategy to Operations for Competitive Advantage.* Harvard Business Publishing, Boston.

Kotter, J.P. (1996) *Leading Change.* Harvard Business Publishing, Boston.

Kotter, J.P., and Cohen, D.S. (2002) *The Heart of Change: Real-Life Stories of How People Change Their Organizations.* Harvard Business Publishing, Boston.

Mankins, M.C., and Steele, R. (2005) Turning Great Strategy into Great Performance. *Harvard Business Review*, 83(7/8), 64-72.

Martin, R.L. (2010) The Execution Trap. *Harvard Business Review*, 88(7/8), 64-71.

McChesney, C., Covey, S., and Huling, J. (2012) *The 4 Disciplines of Execution.* The Free Press, New York.

Mintzberg, H., Pascale, R., Goold, M., and Rumelt, R. (1996) The "Honda Effect" Revisited. *California Management Review,* 38(4), 78-91.

Myers, R. (2001) Budgets on a Roll: Recalculating a Business's Outlook Several Times a Year. *Journal of Accountancy,* 192(6), 41-46.

Sull, D.N. (2007) Closing the Gap Between Strategy and Execution. *MIT Sloan Management Review,* 48(4), 30-38.

Zagotta, R., and Robinson, D. (2002) Keys to Successful Strategy Execution. *Journal of Business Strategy,* 23(1), 30-34.

Chapter 6

Putting It All Together

As mentioned in Chapter 1, organizations need to have a *"comprehensive and integrated management system that links strategy formulation and planning with operational execution"* if they are to be able to successfully formulate, implement and execute their strategy (Kaplan and Norton, 2008, p. 7-8). We call this management system the Formulate and Align to Strategy (FAS) capability.

The literature proposes many best practices that organizations should integrate into their FAS capability (Coon and Wolf, 2005; Hunt, 2006; Kaplan and Norton, 1996, 2005, 2008; Khadem, 2008; Kotter, 1996, 2002; Mankins and Steele, 2005; Martin, 2010; Myers, 2001; Sull, 2007; Zagotta and Robinson, 2002). However, unless business architecture is integrated into it, the FAS capability is impaired and cannot fully alleviate the 10 key issues identified in Chapter 1. The reverse is also true. To generate its full benefits, business architecture must be well integrated into the FAS capability of the organization. The purpose of the resulting business-architecture-enabled FAS (baeFAS) capability is to perform all of the Engage and Govern, Formulate the Strategy, and Implement the Strategy groups of activities identified in Chapter 1. This critical capability should include all of the sub-capabilities, functions, processes, organizational units, know-how assets, information assets and technology assets (information systems in this case) needed to enable the organization to successfully overcome the challenges of formulating and implementing its strategy, as well as overseeing (i.e., monitoring and making decisions that pertain to) the formulation, implementation and execution of that strategy. The baeFAS capability ensures that all of the organization's other capabilities are aligned to its strategy. It does not actually execute the strategy since the organization's strategy can only be truly executed by capabilities such as Design Innovative Products, Market and Sell Products and Services, and Manufacture Products.

The objective of this chapter is to present our reference architecture for the baeFAS capability, describe how this critical capability should function and highlight how business architects should contribute to it. Our reference architecture is designed to enable organizations to effectively and efficiently transform themselves by architecting and implementing their target business architecture (TBA) and target technology architectures (TTAs), executing their transformation plan (TP), and performing the Engage and Govern group of activities described in Chapter 5. It describes the FAS capability as it should be at full maturity, when business architecture is integrated into it. Reaching this level of maturity requires hard work and may take several years. Organizations should use this reference architecture as the starting point for designing the target architecture of their own baeFAS.

Our reference architecture is for single-business-unit organizations or multi-business-unit organizations with a replication or unification operating model (see Chapter 2) that need a single baeFAS for the entire organization. The parent business unit of a multi-business-unit organization with a coordination or diversification operating model and each of its daughter business units should have their own baeFAS capability. They may also need to integrate these capabilities to different degrees depending on several factors such as the operating model chosen, the level of autonomy the parent organization wishes to grant its daughter business units, and the types of synergies that can be generated by linking the strategic plans of these various business units.

This chapter has seven sections, each of which describes the baeFAS capability from one of the following perspectives: sub-capabilities, functions, processes, org units, know-how assets, information assets and technology assets.

Sub-Capabilities

Figure 6.1 depicts all of the sub-capabilities the baeFAS capability should be made up of and the other capabilities of the organization this critical capability must leverage.[1] All of the base building blocks (i.e., functions, processes, org units, know-how assets, information assets and technology assets) required by the baeFAS capability derive from the sub-capabilities shown in this diagram. Where applicable, the oversight activities are embedded in the sub-capabilities that make up the baeFAS capability. For example, the activities required to monitor and decide to adapt the TBA are included in the Architect and Maintain the Business Architecture sub-capability. The work of business architects is central to the sub-capabilities highlighted in dark gray and beneficial to those shown in light gray.

The baeFAS capability is made up of two sub-capabilities: Formulate the Strategy, and Implement and Oversee the Execution of the Strategy. The

---

[1] We could have decomposed the sub-capabilities of the baeFAS capability into even lower-level capabilities. However, such a fine-grained decomposition is not required for the purpose of this chapter.

first sub-capability, Formulate the Strategy, is made up of a number of lower-level capabilities that serve to continuously monitor and assess the external environment; continuously seek new strategic information and insights throughout the organization; assess the organization's capabilities; define and analyze alternative strategies and improvements; and monitor the execution of the strategy. As shown by the dashed arrows in Figure 6.1, some lower-level capabilities of the Formulate the Strategy sub-capability cannot function without the support of other capabilities. For example, the Define and Analyze Alternative Strategies and Improvements lower-level capability must rely on the Elaborate and Maintain the Long-Term Financial Plan sub-capability of the Manage Financial Resources capability to function.

The second sub-capability, Implement and Oversee the Execution of the Strategy, is also made up of a number of lower-level capabilities that serve to architect and maintain the enterprise architecture;[2] identify and sequence transformation projects; manage the execution of the transformation plan; engage stakeholders in the execution of the strategic plan; and monitor the organization's performance. As shown by the dashed arrows in Figure 6.1, the Implement and Oversee the Execution of the Strategy sub-capability also relies on the Transform and Evolve Information Technologies sub-capability of the Operate, Transform and Evolve Information Technologies capability. In addition, some lower-level capabilities of this sub-capability also rely on sub-capabilities of other capabilities. For example, the Manage the Execution of the Transformation Plan sub-capability relies on the Elaborate the Rolling Financial Forecast sub-capability of the Manage Financial Resources Capability.

---

[2] We have deliberately omitted the sub-capabilities that relate to non-IT Target Technology Architectures as those are very dependent on the industry in which the organization operates.

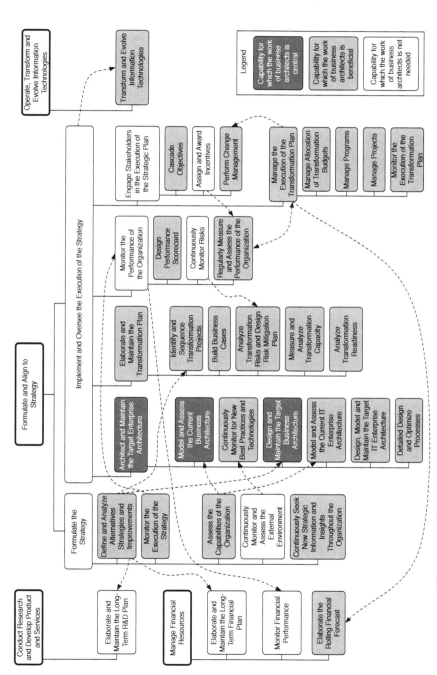

Figure 6.1: Capability network diagram of the Formulate and Align to Strategy capability

Functions

The city map diagram of the business function model (BFM) depicted in Figure 6.2 identifies the functions and sub-functions performed by the baeFAS capability. All sub-functions of the Strategy Formulation, Business Architecture Design and Transformation Planning, Program and Project Management and Enterprise Performance Management functions are shown, whereas only the lower-level functions of the Human Resource Management, Financial Resource Management, Enterprise Risk Management, and IT Management functions that support the baeFAS capability are shown. The main functions performed by business architects are highlighted in dark gray, while those that they should support are shown in medium gray.

Processes

Figure 6.3 depicts the Strategic Assessment-to-Execution Monitoring macro-process at the heart of the baeFAS capability. Although the macro-process may appear complex, most of the processes it is made up of can be found in most organizations, large and small, although they may not always be performed and linked in the way we describe in this chapter.

The macro-process diagram should be read as follows. Each of its processes (rectangular boxes) is identified by its technical name and, in parentheses, common name. As mentioned in Chapter 3, although both technical and common names are provided in the diagram, we prefer to refer to processes by their technical names since their common names are often very similar to those of related capabilities and we want to avoid any possible confusion. Business architects should be key contributors to the processes highlighted in dark gray, but should also contribute, albeit to a lesser extent, to those in medium gray. A circular arrow at the top right corner of a process indicates that it is automatically restarted by its own end or by periodic events (e.g., start of a month). The arrows

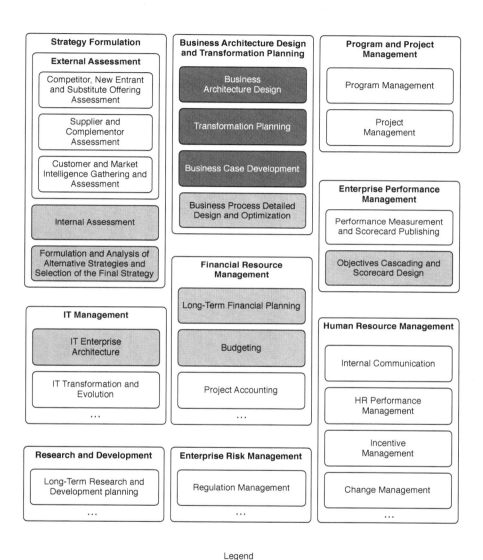

Figure 6.2: Business function model of the
Formulate and Align to Strategy capability

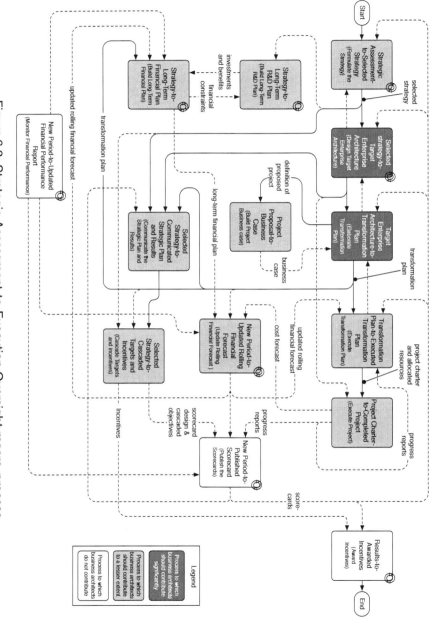

Figure 6.3: Strategic Assessment-to-Execution Oversight macro-process

connecting processes represent information flows between those processes. They show that the outputs of one process (at the arrow tail) are the inputs of another process (at the arrowhead). To avoid making the diagram overly complex, only the main information flows are shown in Figure 6.3. A solid arrow arriving at the left side of a process represents an input whose arrival triggers the execution of this process. A dashed arrow arriving at a process represents an input that is required by the process but that does not trigger its execution. An arrow leaving from either side of a process represents an output that this process makes available to another process once it is completed, while an arrow leaving a process from the bottom represents a request this process makes to another process, a response to which is needed before the first process can be completed (represented using another arrow arriving at the process that made the request).

The macro-process starts with the Strategic Assessment-to-Selected Strategy process, which is described in detail in Chapter 2. The purpose of this process is to formulate and continuously improve the organization's strategy. It includes four activities, namely the assessment of organization's internal environment, the assessment of the external environment, the formulation and analysis of alternative strategies (which includes the outline of their respective long-term R&D plan, TEA, TP and long-term financial plan), and finally the selection and codification of the final strategy.

The purposes of the second and third processes, Strategy-to-Long-term R&D Plan and Strategy-to-Long-Term Financial Plan, are to respectively create the long-term R&D and financial plans for the next three to five years. Once a strategy has been selected and its corresponding TP has been fully elaborated, both of these processes are executed to produce the long-term financial and R&D plans. Thereafter, these processes are re-executed once a year to update the long-term R&D and long-term financial plans. These updates are required to account for the latest information available and to extend these plans by another year.

The purpose of the fourth process, Selected Strategy-to-Target Enterprise Architecture is to define how the organization and its technology assets must function in the future so the organization can execute its strategy in full. The inputs for this process are the selected strategy and the TEA outline created during the Strategic Assessment-to-Selected Strategy process. As mentioned in Chapter 1, the TEA includes the TBA, the target IT enterprise architecture (TITEA) and possibly other target technology architectures (TTAs). Because of the large amount of work required to architect a complete TEA in all but the smallest of organizations, the TEA architecture effort should be divided into increments that each focus on one or a few slices of the organization at a time. Such an incremental approach implies that the Selected Strategy-to-Target Enterprise Architecture process must be iterative (i.e., repeated for every new increment) and that the order in which the slices are architected must be based on their importance to the implementation of the strategy. Each iteration must also take into account changes made to the strategy, the introduction of new technologies, and other new insights gained and information learned by the organization. The Selected Strategy-to-Target Enterprise Architecture process also includes the modeling of the current enterprise architecture (CEA) the first time a slice of the TEA is architected.

The purpose of the fifth process, Target Enterprise Architecture-to-Transformation Plan, is to define, select and sequence all of the transformation projects that the organization must execute during the next three to five years to implement parts or all of its TEA. As mentioned in Chapter 4, the TP should select transformation projects based on whether or not they are essential to the implementation of the strategy; the dependencies that exist between the projects; and the projects' benefits, resource requirements, and risks. This process can provide feedback to the Selected Strategy-to-Target Enterprise Architecture process so the TEA can be adjusted when necessary (e.g., when the benefits of some transformations are not sufficient to justify them).

The sixth process, Project Proposal-to-Business Case, is initiated by the Target Enterprise Architecture-to-Transformation Plan process. Its purpose is to identify the pros and cons of executing a particular project. As mentioned in Chapter 4, a business case should, in addition to determining whether a project is essential or optional to the execution of the strategy, identify the objectives, tangible and intangible benefits, resource requirements, risks, and the extended organization's readiness and capacity to execute it. The outputs of the Project Proposal-to-Business Case process are used by the Target Enterprise Architecture-to-Transformation Plan process to select and prioritize projects.

The seventh process, Selected Strategy-to-Communicated Strategic Plan and Results, has two purposes: first, to communicate the strategic plan and ensure that a critical mass of members working at all levels throughout the organization understand it properly and buy into it; second, to communicate the results achieved as the TP and the strategy are executed. This process should use the information from the Strategic Assessment-to-Selected Strategy, Selected Strategy-to-Target Enterprise Architecture, Target Enterprise Architecture-to-Transformation Plan and New Period-to-Published Scorecard processes as inputs. As mentioned in Chapter 5, communication should be two-way, frequent and sustained so that all stakeholders are motivated and momentum is built and maintained throughout the formulation, implementation and execution of the strategy.

The purpose of the eight process, Selected Strategy-to-Cascaded Targets and Incentives is to cascade the objectives down the entire organizational structure to create individual targets for personnel and, if the organization so choses, tie incentives to the achievement of these targets. A key activity in this process is the design and maintenance of a scorecard that will be used to report on the achievement of all targets. The targets to be included in the scorecard should be those defined in the strategic plan and in the business cases of the transformation projects included in the TP. Whenever changes are made to the strategic plan, the Selected Strategy-to-Cascaded Targets and Incentives process should be triggered so any necessary adjustments can be made to the cascaded targets and their associated incentives.

The ninth process, Project Charter-to-Completed Project, is required to execute the transformations identified in a given project charter (i.e., to execute a given project). This process is repeated as many times as there are projects to be executed. Since each project is unique, the sequence and nature of the activities that make up the Project Charter-to-Completed Project process are different every time the process is executed. Nonetheless, this process encompasses four phases: (1) project initiation; (2) project planning; (3) transformation execution; and (4) project closing. It includes the detailed design, development, testing and implementation of the transformations as well as all related project management, project accounting and change management activities required to successfully achieve the objectives set for the project. It also includes the updating of the CEA models and documentation to reflect the transformations executed by the project. The Strategic Assessment-to-Selected Strategy and Selected Strategy-to-Target Enterprise Architecture processes use these new models as input the next time they are executed.

The purpose of the tenth process, Transformation Plan-to-Executed Transformation Plan, is to oversee the execution of the TP. This process initiates projects according to the TP and allocates resources to them. It also routinely monitors the progress made by ongoing projects and, when necessary, helps them resolve issues as they come up. The Transformation Plan-to-Executed Transformation Plan process does not directly execute transformations; instead, it serves as the "control tower" that orchestrates the execution of the TP. This process provides feedback to the Target Enterprise Architecture-to-Transformation Plan process so adjustments can be made when needed. As mentioned in Chapter 5, this process should use a stage-gate approach to fund transformation projects. Each project should be reviewed at a predefined set of three or four predefined milestones (i.e., gates) before it is funded to progress to the next gate (i.e., before the next stage is funded).

The purpose of the eleventh process, New Period-to-Updated Financial Performance Report, is to monitor the organization's financial performance. This process provides feedback to the Strategy-to-Long-Term Financial Plan, New Period-to-Updated Rolling Financial Forecast and New Period-to-Published Scorecard processes.

The purpose of the twelfth process, New Period-to-Updated Rolling Financial Forecast, is to produce a new rolling financial forecast every month or quarter. This process uses inputs such as the long-term financial plan, the TP, the latest cost forecasts from the projects and the financial performance reports. The New Period-to-Updated Rolling Financial Forecast process also uses several other inputs such as sales and production forecasts, which are not shown in Figure 6.3 as they are the outputs of processes other than the Strategic Assessment-to-Execution Monitoring macro-process. It is important to mention here that the New Period-to-Updated Rolling Financial Forecast process is not the process that funds projects. Instead, it sets a global transformation budget, which is then used by the Transformation Plan-to-Executed Transformation Plan process to fund individual projects.

The purpose of the thirteenth process, New Period-to-Published Scorecard, is to measure the results of the execution of the strategic plan and to publish these results on a scorecard at least on a monthly basis. The information included in this scorecard is then used by other processes, including many of the ones in the Strategic Assessment-to-Execution Monitoring macro-process, to identify issues that must be addressed or successful actions that hopefully can be repeated.

The fourteenth and last process, Results-to-Awarded Incentives, uses the results published in the scorecard to assess to what extent strategic objectives have been met and to determine what proportion of the promised incentives should be granted to each member of the organization.

Org Units

One vertical structure and four horizontal organizational structures must be put in place for the baeFAS capability to function properly. These structures are described in the following subsections.

Vertical Organizational Structure

For the baeFAS capability to deliver the value it promises, highly effective and efficient coordination is required between the various business functions that it relies upon. This requires that organizations create an Office of Strategy Management (OSM) responsible for coordinating and making recommendations (not decisions) on matters pertaining to the formulation, implementation and execution of the strategy. The OSM is not responsible for overseeing the formulation, implementation and execution of the strategy. These oversight duties should be held by the four governance boards described later in this chapter. The OSM is, however, responsible for gathering the monitoring information required by the four governance boards to perform their oversight duties. The OSM should be led by the organization's chief strategy officer (CSO). The name of this org unit, Office of Strategy Management, comes from Kaplan and Norton (2005). However, as described below, we think the OSM should be given more responsibilities than they suggest.

The OSM should be divided into six lower-level org units: the Strategy Office, the Business Architecture Office, the Transformation Project Management Office, the Enterprise Performance Management Office, the Change Management Support Office and the Business Process Management Office. The business functions each of these offices is responsible for are shown in Figure 6.4.

The Strategy Office is responsible for the assessment of the external and internal environments, the formulation and analysis of alternative strategies, and the recommendation of one of these alternatives to the CSO, who in turn should recommend it to the Strategy Governance Board (described later in this chapter). The Business Architecture Office (BAO) is responsible for architecting the TBA, elaborating the TP, and building the business case for each of the transformation projects. The Transformation Project Management Office[3] (TPMO) is responsible for managing transformation projects and programs. This org unit should include all of the project and program managers working on transformation projects. The Enterprise Performance Management Office (EPMO) is responsible for supporting executives and other leaders in cascading targets down the entire organizational structure, designing scorecards, measuring results, and publishing the scorecards.

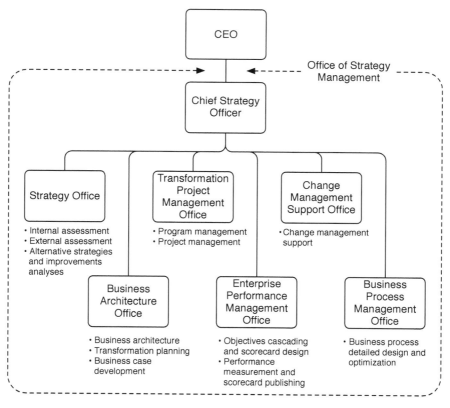

Figure 6.4: Organizational chart of the OSM

---

[3]   Not to be confused with the typical IT PMOs common to many organizations.

The role of the Change Management Support Office (CMSO) is to support and coach the guiding coalition in leading change throughout the organization. This support and coaching is necessary because members of the guiding coalition often do not have the necessary fine-tuned leadership skills nor enough time to allocate to the critical task of leading change throughout the implementation of the the strategy. The CMSO should comprise a few professionals who are highly skilled at conducting stakeholder analyses, and at planning and creating communications that are effective in creating a sense of urgency and getting people to understand and buy into the strategic plan and commit to its execution. The members of the CMSO should also be accustomed to working with executives. The CMSO should not be responsible for managing training or creating procedures. These functions should remain the responsibility of other org units such as HR. Adding these functions to the CMSO would distract its members from their real purpose.

Finally, the Business Process Management Office should support projects in transforming processes and assist leaders across the organization as they continuously work on improving the effectiveness and efficiency of the processes they are responsible for. This office should be staffed with business process reengineering and improvement professionals trained in methods such as Six Sigma, Lean and the Theory of Constraints.

Depending on the size of the organization, one or more managers may be required to manage the six offices that make up the OSM. Indeed, in small organizations, the staff of all of these org units could report directly to the CSO, while in large organizations a dedicated manager may be needed for each of the six lower-level offices.

The business case development function should be assigned to the BAO because, in addition to ensuring that business cases are built in a uniform fashion, it ensures that they are built from the perspective of the whole organization and not from that of individual org units. Conversely, when the managers of each org unit are responsible for developing their own business cases, it is difficult for them to account for the positive and negative impacts the transformations they are proposing will have on other org units. There are three reasons for this. First, they seldom have the necessary understanding of the functioning of the organization as a whole to identify all of the org units that may be impacted by the transformations they are proposing. Second, they rarely analyze the impacts the transformations they propose will have on other org units because it requires more effort than they are willing to invest in building their business cases. Third, they may be reluctant to become accountable for benefits that can only be achieved if transformations are also made in other org units. Not taking into account the positive and negative impacts the transformations proposed for one org unit can have on other org units has two important negative consequences for the organization. First, worthwhile transformation projects are often abandoned because they are difficult to justify without accounting for the positive impacts they may have on other org units, while other projects are approved despite the unaccounted for negative impacts they will have on other org units. Second, the transformations that are proposed are mostly only local optimizations and not transformations that can generate important benefits for the organization as a whole. Even though the BAO should play an important role in developing business cases for all proposed transformation projects, it is important for the managers and subject matter experts (SMEs) of the org units that will be impacted by these projects to be involved in preparing these business cases. In addition, accountants should be involved in the preparation of business cases to ensure that they abide by proper accounting practices.

The IT Enterprise Architecture Office and related functions are not included within the OSM for two reasons. First, the skill set required to architect the TITEA comprises mostly IT skills. Second, most chief information officers would understandably object to people outside their org unit deciding how their team should build information systems. All that is needed is close collaboration between the members of the BAO and the IT Enterprise

Architecture Office to ensure that the information system transformations are designed to properly enable the business transformations set out in the TBA. For similar reasons, the offices responsible for the other TTAs of the organization are not included within the OSM.

Having an OSM can provide three important benefits to the firm. First, it clarifies the leadership of the baeFAS capability and assigns it to a single executive rather than diffusing this leadership and accountability amongst several executives. Thus, baeFAS capability related decision-making is simplified and accelerated. Second, it enables the OSM's six offices to share the same priorities and to be protected from priorities other than those of formulating, implementing and monitoring the execution of the strategy. Third, but not least, it facilitates communication, coordination and collaboration between the OSM's offices by virtue of its simple management hierarchy. To actually reap the benefits of this simple management hierarchy, however, it is imperative that the six offices of the OSM forge strong collaborative relationships with each other and with other org units in the organization. For example, the Strategy Office must rely on the marketing team to gather the market and customer intelligence needed to assess the external environment and identify new business opportunities. The Strategy Office must also collaborate with the BAO to assess the internal environment and analyze alternative strategies and improvement opportunities. The BAO, in turn, must work very closely with the various org units that will be impacted by the transformations, as well as with the IT Enterprise Architecture Office, the TPMO and the EPMO. Both the BAO and the TPMO must work very closely with experts in the IT org unit since most business transformations today are enabled by information systems transformations.

Horizontal Organizational Structures

The OSM must be complemented with four horizontal organizational structures – committees in this case – to ensure sound decision-making with regard to the formulation, implementation and execution of the strategy: (1) the Strategy Governance Board (SGB); (2) the Transformation Governance Board (TGB); (3) the Transformation Project Management Board (TPMB); and (4) the Architecture Review Board (ARB). The following paragraphs describe the purpose of each of these committees, how they should function, their typical membership and their associated decision-making roles. The makeup of the committees presented below is for illustrative purposes only. Indeed, because the correct membership of each committee depends greatly on the particular organization's structure, it is not possible to present a definitive list of members for any of the four committees. As discussed in Chapter 3, we use the RAPID framework to identify the decision-making roles the members of each committee should have. The **R** in RAPID stands for Recommender. The person who has this role is responsible for making the recommendation. People who have the **A** role (Agree) have veto power over the recommendation, but not the decision. People with the **P** role (Perform) are responsible for carrying out the decision once it has been made. The people who have the **I** role (Input) are responsible for providing inputs used in building the recommendation. Finally, the person who has the **D** role (Decide) is accountable for making the decision once the recommendation is made. This person can modify or overrule the recommendation.

Strategy Governance Board

The SGB is the executive-level committee accountable for the formulation of the strategy and the oversight of its execution. The SGB reports to the board of directors, which owns the business strategy on behalf of the organization's shareholders. The SGB should hold two types of meetings. The purpose of the first type is to make decisions that pertain to the formulation and updating of the strategy. Initially, these meetings are used to consider possible strategy alternatives in preparation for making a recommendation to the board of directors. Once a strategy has been selected and set in motion, these meetings are used to improve the strategy when necessary. During these quarterly or annual meetings, the committee reviews and attempts to make sense of the latest information related to the macro-environment factors (i.e., political, legal, economic, social, technological, ecological and climatic, and infrastructure environments) and the six industry competitive forces (competitors, new entrants, customers, suppliers, substitutes and complementors), and assesses how the owners, customers, partners and employees are responding to the strategy.

The purpose of the second type of meeting is to monitor how the execution of the strategy is progressing, learn from the latest outcomes and issues, and make any necessary adjustments to the execution of the strategy. These meetings should be held at least monthly – even more frequently when necessary.

A typical SGB should include the chief executive officer (CEO), chief strategy officer (CSO), chief operating officer (COO), chief marketing officer (CMO), chief financial officer (CFO), chief compliance officer (CCO), chief information officer (CIO), chief human resources officer (CHRO), and possibly other executives depending on the size of the organization and the industry within which it operates. A few additional people with key expertise could also be invited to join the SGB. We recommend that decision-making roles within the SGB be assigned along the lines shown in Table 6.1.

Transformation Governance Board

The TGB is the executive-level committee accountable for the implementation of the strategy. It is accountable, but not responsible, for the creation and evolution of the TEA and TP, and for overseeing the implementation of the TEA and execution of the TP. The TGB complements the SGB: it focuses on the implementation of the strategy while the SGB attends to issues that relate to its formulation and execution. The members of the TGB and SGB are often identical, but may differ somewhat. We recommend that decision-making roles within the TGB be assigned along the lines shown in Table 6.1.

Transformation Project Management Board

The TPMB is responsible for overseeing the execution of the projects included in the TP. Its purpose is twofold. First, it regularly reviews transformation projects' costs, timelines and risks, and supports project managers in resolving issues that arise. Second, it manages the project funding stage-gate process (as discussed in Chapter 5). A transformation project that reaches a gate should only be funded to proceed to the next gate if it has received a positive review from the ARB (described later in this chapter). A typical TPMB should include the CSO, the head of the BAO, the head of the TPMO and a manager from finance. The heads of the IT Enterprise Architecture Office and the IT Project Management Office should also be members of the TPMB because, as mentioned above, most business transformations depend on corresponding

Table 6.1: Typical assignment of decision-making roles within the Strategy Governance Board and the Transformation Governance Board

Person	Decision-making roles	
	SGB	TGB
Chief executive officer	Decide	Decide
Chief strategy officer	Recommend (strategy and its execution)	Recommend (business architecture and transformation plan), Agree (IT enterprise architecture)
Chief operating officer	Input, Agree, Perform	Input, Agree, Perform
Chief financial officer	Input	Input
Chief marketing officer	Input, Agree, Perform	Input, Perform
Chief human resources officer	Input, Perform	Input, Perform
Chief compliance officer	Input	Input
Chief information officer	Input, Perform	Input, Perform, Recommend (IT enterprise architecture)
Subject matter experts	Input	Input

information systems transformations. The TPMB's decision-making rights should be set by the TGB. We recommend that decision-making roles within the TPMB be assigned in a similar way to that shown in Table 6.2.

Although this may appear strange at first glance, the head of the Business Architecture Office (HBAO) should have the Recommend role in the TPMB. Because the TP has been prepared by the HBAO's team, he or she is the person best placed to recommend adjustments to it. Giving anybody else the Recommend role on the TPMB would mean that nobody is really responsible for the elaboration and evolution TP. In addition, giving the HBAO the Recommend role ensures that projects are reviewed by the ARB (described below) at each gate and that all ARB-identified architecture issues are resolved before the TPMB approves them to proceed with the next stage. However, when difficult issues arise, they may need to be raised with the TGB. In turn, the head of the IT Enterprise Architecture Office has an Agree role in the TPMB because of his/her Decide role on the ARB. The heads of the TPMO and IT Project Management Office have Input roles with regard to the organization's current readiness and capacity to successfully execute the projects the HBAO recommends. The job of the CSO, who has the Decide role in the TPMB, is to balance the organization's desire to transform itself rapidly and its desire to create the ideal conditions before initiating a given project.

Table 6.2: Typical assignment of decision-making roles within the Transformation Project Management Board

Person	Decision-making roles
Chief strategy officer	Decide
Head of Business Architecture Office	Recommend
Head of Transformation Project Management Office	Input, Perform
Head of IT Enterprise Architecture Office	Input, Agree
Head of IT Project Management Office	Input, Perform
Manager from Finance	Input

<u>Architecture Review Board</u>

The ARB monitors the implementation of the TEA by transformation projects and reviews and resolves any scope or architecture issues that arise during the execution of these projects. If you question the need for a committee like the ARB, ask yourself if you would let a group of contractors, each responsible for a different part of a $100-million bridge, work without setting up a governance body to oversee their work as it progresses, ensure that it is in agreement with the engineering plans, and review all proposed changes before they are authorized. Left to their own devices, the contractors would likely make changes that, although reasonable from their own perspective, cause difficulties for other contractors and result in a bridge that does not meet all requirements set for it at the onset of its construction and may even be structurally unsound. The teams working on the different transformation projects included in an organization's TP are just like those bridge-building contractors. Although they play an essential role in building the organization of the future, if they are not supported by an ARB, they are likely to execute transformations that do not fit together or do not meet all of the organization's requirements.

A typical ARB should include the HBAO, the head of the IT Enterprise Architecture Office, and a number of business architects, IT enterprise architects and other SMEs. Indeed, although the ARB must include managers, it should also include professionals whose role is to provide information and advise the managers. Managers cannot assume the responsibilities of the ARB on their own. They simply do not have the time nor, in most cases, the inclination and expertise needed to go into the details of the TEA and TP. They need professionals to help them do this. The decision rights of the ARB should be set by the TGB. We recommend that decision-making roles within the ARB be assigned in a similar manner to that shown in Table 6.3.

The ARB should not act as a police force whose ultimate objective is to enforce the TEA no matter what. On the contrary, it should value the inputs it receives from the transformation project teams, which are made up of intelligent people trying to do the right thing for the organization. These teams face significant challenges that sometimes stimulate them to come up with bright new ideas that may be beneficial for the organization but require project scope or TEA changes before they can be implemented. Hence, the best way to empower project teams and avoid slowing them down is to designate a group of senior professionals to assist them in finding solutions for the issues they face while considering the impacts these solutions may have outside of their projects. Although the types and number of professionals included in this group depend on the nature of the project, it generally includes business architects, IT enterprise architects and sometimes professionals responsible for other TTAs. Before a project reaches a gate, this designated group should write a brief report for the ARB. This report should indicate if the project is proposing to deviate from its original mandate or TEA and, if so, describe the deviations and make a recommendation as to whether or not accept them. With this method, only project teams proposing deviations should come before the ARB.

Table 6.3: Typical assignment of decision-making
roles within the Architecture Review Board

Person	Decision-making roles
Head of Business Architecture Office	Decide (bus. arch.)
Head of IT Enterprise Architecture Office	Decide (IT ent. arch.)
Business architect	Recommend (bus. arch.), Input (IT ent. arch.)
IT enterprise architect	Recommend (IT ent. arch.), Input (bus. arch.)
Representative from IT systems development	Input, Perform
Representative from IT Infrastructure and operations	Input, Perform
Representative from IT security	Input, Agree

Know-how

In order to function properly, the baeFAS capability requires specific know-how so it can successfully perform the tasks below. Although business architects should have a fair understanding of all of these areas, they should be especially well versed in the seven areas preceded by a star:

★ assess the internal environment;

• assess the external environment;

★ define, analyze and codify alternative strategies;

• model the current business architecture;

• model the current IT enterprise architecture;

★ design, model and document the TBA;

• design, model and document the TITEA;

★ elaborate the transformation plan;

★ build business cases;

★ identify and analyze transformation risks;

★ analyze transformation readiness and capacity;

• cascade targets down all levels throughout the organization;

• design incentive programs;

• manage performance;

• create and execute communication programs;

• manage change;

• design a scorecard;

• manage programs and projects;

- elaborate a long-term financial plan; and

- elaborate a rolling financial forecast.

In addition to the types of know-how listed above, the baeFAS capability requires in-depth know-how specific to the capabilities of the organization that need to be transformed. This specific know-how includes insights generated internally, in-depth knowledge of industry best practices and other know-how acquired externally. This know-how should be provided by internal and external SMEs.

Information

The baeFAS capability requires the following types of information to function properly:

- external environment assessment;

- internal environment assessment;

- value, mission and vision;

- stakeholder value propositions (i.e., owner value proposition, customer value proposition, partner value proposition and employee value proposition);

★ business constraints (i.e., policies, guidelines, regulations and standards);

★ goals, objectives and targets;

★ current and target business architectures;

- current and target technology architectures;

★ business architecture gaps;

- technology architecture gaps;

★ transformation plan;

★ three perspectives of the organizational context (i.e., locations, customer segments, products and services);

★ best practices and related benchmarks;

★ risks and controls;

★ work packages, projects and programs;

★ project charters;

★ project business cases;

★ strategic and business transformation assumptions; and

· long-term financial plan and rolling financial forecast.

Business architects should contribute to the creation of the 12 information types that are preceded by a star. The sum of these 12 information types, together with the current and target technology architectures and the technology architecture gaps, forms what we call the enterprise architecture information base (EAIB). The EAIB is a purely descriptive information base. It describes the organization as it is today and as it should be in the future, the transformations that must be executed and the objectives that motivate these transformations. This information is fundamental to the work of numerous professionals in an organization. Strategists, business architects, IT architects, project and program managers, governance, risk and compliance (GRC) analysts, business process improvement professionals, business continuity analysts and enterprise performance management analysts should all participate in building and maintaining this knowledge base. All of these professionals should contribute to the EAIB by making the information they create available to others so they can leverage it and avoid re-creating it.

Technologies

A number of technology assets must be put to work for the baeFAS capability to function at its best. They include three important information systems: the enterprise architecture information base management system (EAIBMS), enterprise project portfolio management information system (EPPMIS) and enterprise performance management information system (EPMIS).

An EAIBMS is a central repository to capture and maintain the shared EAIB described above. It contains and helps to manage the "single version of the truth" that many types of professionals across the organization create and need to share with each other so they can work more coherently and efficiently. The EAIBMS should be used to build and continuously maintain the EAIB as the organization evolves over time. For example, once a revised process has been stored in the EAIBMS by the process improvement professional who drafted it, a GRC analyst can immediately analyze its inherent risks, design the necessary control activities to mitigate them and save this new information in the EAIBMS. In the meantime, an IT architect can analyze the proposed process changes, identify the information systems modifications required to enable them, and save this information in the EAIBMS. Other people can also be given full or partial access to the EAIBMS. For example, employees could consult the maps of the current processes to better understand how their work is connected to the organization's other activities.

In addition to serving as a central repository, the EAIBMS should provide at least the following features for the organization:

★ Strategic plan codification;

★ Business architecture modeling and documentation;

★ Process modeling and simulation;

- • IT enterprise and systems architecture modeling and documenting;

- ★ Information and data modeling and documenting;

- • Operational risks and controls modeling and documenting;[4]

- • Business continuity analysis; and

- ★ Roadmapping.[5]

Again, the five functionalities preceded by a star are those that business architects typically use.

An EPPMIS enables the organization to holistically manage its portfolio of projects and programs. It should provide at least the following features for the organization:

- • Detailed project and program planning;

- • Detailed project and program tracking;

- • Program and project budget management;

- • Capacity planning;

- • Resource assignment;

- • Project time sheets; and

- • Project status reporting.

It is important to mention here that the TP should be created in the EAIBMS and not in the EPPMIS. The reason for this is that the models of the CEA and TEA, the enterprise architecture gaps and all the strategic plan objectives are already captured in the EAIBMS, and the EAIBMS is the only information system capable of capturing the links between these items and the work packages, projects and programs included in the TP.

---

[4] Does not include audit and evidence management.

[5] Not to be confused with detailed planning of programs and projects.

An EPMIS automates performance measurement and scorecarding.[6] It should provide at least the following features:

- Scorecard definition and cascading;

- Scorecard data gathering;

- Scorecard publication; and

- Scorecard collaboration (enabling people to capture and share comments on the results presented in the scorecard).

---

[6] Not to be confused with other information systems, also known as EPMIS, which provide functionalities such as financial planning, budgeting, financial period closing and financial consolidation.

References

Coon, B., and Wolf, S. (2005) The Alchemy of Strategy Execution. *Employment Relations Today*, 32(3), 19-30.

Hunt, S. (2006) *Building Finance and Performance Management Mastery with Superior Budgeting and Forecasting Capabilities.* Accenture.

Kaplan, R.S., and Norton, D.P. (1996) *The Balanced Scorecard: Translating Strategy into Action.* Harvard Business Publishing, Boston.

Kaplan, R.S., and Norton, D.P. (2005) The Office of Strategy Management. *Harvard Business Review*, 83(10), 72-80.

Kaplan, R.S., and Norton, D.P. (2008) *The Execution Premium: Linking Strategy to Operations for Competitive Advantage.* Harvard Business Publishing, Boston.

Khadem, R. (2008) Alignment and Follow-Up: Steps to Strategy Execution. *Journal of Business Strategy*, 29(6), 29-35.

Kotter, J.P. (1996) *Leading Change.* Harvard Business Publishing, Boston.

Kotter, J.P. (2002) *The Heart of Change: Real-Life Stories of How People Change Their Organizations.* Harvard Business Publishing, Boston.

Mankins, M.C., and Steele, R. (2005) Turning Great Strategy into Great Performance. *Harvard Business Review*, 83(7/8), 64-72.

Martin, R. (2010) The Execution Trap. *Harvard Business Review*, 83(7/8), 64-72.

Myers, R. (2001) Budgets on a Roll: Recalculating a Business's Outlook Several Times a Year. *Journal of Accountancy*, 192(6), 41-46.

Sull, D.N. (2007) Closing the Gap Between Strategy and Execution. *MIT Sloan Management Review*, 48(4), 30-38.

Zagotta, R., and Robinson, D. (2002) Keys to Successful Strategy Execution. *Journal of Business Strategy*, 23(1), 30-34.

Chapter 7

Leadership Agenda

In the first six chapters of this book, we described what business architecture is (i.e., the target business architecture (TBA), transformation plan (TP) and business architecture practice), identified the benefits it can provide, presented numerous contributions business architects can make to the strategic endeavors of their organizations, and presented our reference architecture for the business-architecture-enabled Formulate and Align to Strategy (baeFAS) capability. The objective of this concluding chapter is to lay out the leadership agenda for organizations that want to adopt business architecture and integrate it into their FAS capability. This chapter has two sections, the first of which presents the three key business-architecture-related leadership principles organizations must abide by, while the second presents the first set of activities leaders should initiate, contribute to and oversee to start integrating business architecture into their FAS capability and creating their organization's TBA and TP.

Business-Architecture-Related Leadership Principles

Leaders who wish to adopt business architecture and integrate it into their organization's FAS capability should abide by the following key business-architecture-related leadership principles:

1. Lead from the top

2. Foster collaboration

3. Proceed incrementally

These key principles overarch the numerous guidelines put forth throughout the earlier chapters of this book.

Lead from the top

Top executives must provide leadership in integrating business architecture into their organization's FAS capability. This integration requires, amongst other things, process and organizational architecture transformations that impact the executives themselves as well as many other senior managers. Top executives must also provide leadership in creating the TBA and the TP, in adapting these plans over time and in leveraging them to govern the implementation of their organization's strategy. Executives must decide in which order the slices of the TBA will be architected, must ensure that all the right stakeholders contribute to their creation, and must involve themselves in architecting this plan and elaborating the corresponding TP so they can understand the key issues identified, help make hard choices and buy into the resulting TBA and TP themselves. Once these plans have been created, executives must continue to provide leadership by seeking buy-in and commitment to the TBA and TP from all members of the organization. As discussed in Chapter 5, executives must also provide strong leadership in monitoring the implementation of the TBA and execution of the TP in order to remove barriers hampering progress and see to their adaptation when necessary.

Finally, executives must hold themselves and other stakeholders accountable for achieving the targets set in the TP. All of this leadership can only be provided by the executives at the top of the organization. We have seen very talented people in other positions try to substitute themselves for these executives in this leadership role. They all failed. They simply did not have the necessary clout.

Foster collaboration

Fostering collaboration across the organization is critical for the integration of business architecture into the FAS capability, and for the effective and efficient creation and execution of the TBA and TP. There are several important reasons for this. First, many people must change how they work in order to integrate business architecture into their organization's FAS capability and, without their collaboration, successful integration cannot be achieved. Second, the TBA and TP cannot be the work of just one or a few people, however talented they may be, because of the range of expertise required and because that would make it difficult to get people throughout the organization to buy into these plans prior to their execution. Finally, the TP cannot be successfully executed without the collaboration of all stakeholders affected.

Proceed incrementally

Leaders should integrate business architecture into their organization's FAS capability incrementally. Indeed, because reaching the level of maturity corresponding to the reference architecture presented in Chapter 6 requires that major transformations be made to the organization's culture and building blocks, it is far better to spread these transformations out over time and give each one the necessary time to become entrenched in the organization's functioning before further transformations are executed.

As mentioned in previous chapters, organizations should also proceed incrementally to create their TBA and TP. That is because architecting the complete TBA and corresponding TP for today's complex organizations often takes many years, but competitive pressures do not grant organizations the luxury of waiting so long before they start transforming themselves. It is therefore, as mentioned above, imperative that leaders divide their organization into slices and that the TBA of each of these slices be architected in the order of their strategic importance, each time updating the TP so it covers all of the slices architected so far. This iterative process ensures that organizations can rapidly start using their TBA and TP to guide their transformation even though these plans are still incomplete.

Getting Started

As mentioned in Chapter 1, to generate its full potential benefits, business architecture must be well integrated into the organization's FAS capability. For this integration to work and reach the level of maturity corresponding to the reference architecture presented in Chapter 6, leaders should adopt an incremental approach. The number of steps that must be taken and the number of things that must be done at each step to build a baeFAS capability depend, amongst other things, on the current state of the FAS capability and the organization's internal politics. However, leaders should ensure that the first step includes the following sequence of activities.

1. Assess the organization's readiness

    First, leaders must assess the organization's readiness in order to identify the challenges that face the integration of business architecture into the organization's FAS capability and the means by which these challenges can be overcome.

2. Create awareness

    Leaders must then create awareness of business architecture. Creating this awareness is essential because executives, managers and other stakeholders generally are not aware of what business architecture is and what benefits it can provide to the organization. Bringing in external experts to participate in this activity is often the most effective way of creating such awareness.

3. Identify the first slice of the organization to be architected

    Leaders should identify the first slice of the organization to be architected. This slice should address the challenges faced by executives and managers who have bought into the idea of business architecture during the awareness creation activity.

4. Secure funding

    Once the first slice has been identified, funding must be secured for the efforts that will be made to architect this slice and elaborate the corresponding TP.

5. Secure talent

    Leaders must secure business architecture talent. This can be done by training people with high potential who are already part of the organization, by hiring from outside the organization, or by relying on the help of one or more consultants to get started. The selected individuals should be (not in order of importance) fast learners, innovators, leaders, strategic thinkers, intensely curious, internally driven, team players, great communicators and good modelers.

6. Create the first slice's TBA and TP

    Business architects should architect the TBA of the organization's first slice and elaborate the corresponding TP. Obviously, this activity should be executed in collaboration with relevant leaders and stakeholders.

    Since executives and other stakeholders are probably not yet completely convinced of the benefits business architecture can give their organization, this architecture effort must deliver value quickly in order to get their full buy-in. To do this, only the sub-architectures that are most helpful in surmounting the challenges at hand should be architected during this activity.

7. Showcase success

Once the first slice's TBA and TP have been created, they should be showcased to executives and other stakeholders across the organization together with the benefits the execution of the TP and implementation of the TBA are expected to provide for the organization. The TBA and TP should be showcased in collaboration with the executives and managers who contributed to the creation of this first slice.

It is important to mention here that the value of business architecture must be well recognized throughout the organization before leaders decide to take the next step in their effort to integrate business architecture into their organization's FAS capability. Achieving this recognition, in turn, may require some of the above activities to be performed several times.

Glossary

Term	Definition
Activity	Either a sub-process or a task.
Aggregate capability	A capability made up of either two or more lower-level aggregate capabilities or two or more base capabilities.
Artifact	"An object made by a human being" (*New Oxford American Dictionary*).
Assumption	Things accepted as true without proof and over which the organization has little or no control.
Atomic capability	A capability that is made up of base building blocks and cannot be decomposed into lower-level capabilities
Atomic function	A function that cannot be decomposed any further.
baeFAS	A Formulate and Align to Strategy capability enabled by business architecture.
Base building block	A business capability, business function, business process, org unit, know-how asset, information asset, brand, technology asset or natural resource deposit.
Brand	A name and/or logo associated with a number of products and/or services to distinguish them from other similar products and/or services, and to convey that these products and/or services share important customer value proposition attributes.
Building block	Any resource of which an organization is made up and which can be transformed (e.g., business processes, organizational units, IT systems, production facilities).
Building block transformation	Any lasting change (i.e., acquisition/creation, modification or sale/retirement) made to an individual building block of the organization.
Business architecture	The sum of the target business architecture, the transformation plan and the business architecture practice.
Business architecture building block	A business capability, business function, business process, org unit, know-how asset, information asset or brand.

Term	Definition
Business capability	An integrated set of building blocks designed to work together to attain a specific result.
Business constraint	A regulation, standard, policy or guideline.
Business function	A kind of work done by the organization.
Business model	The "rationale of how an organization creates, delivers, and captures value" (Osterwalder and Pigneur, 2010, p. 14).
Business process	"A set of activities, methods, and practices that transforms a set of inputs into a set of products and services" (Object Management Group, 2008, p. 463).
Business unit	An organizational unit (org unit) that has its own profit and loss statements and possibly even its own legal standing.
Catalog	A special type of table that contains a list of items with their descriptions and possibly other information about them.
Classification relationship	A relationship that exists between two building blocks when one is a type of the other.
Committee	An org unit made up of people from different vertical org units who are appointed to work together to make decisions on a specific matter and coordinate related activities. It may be permanent or temporary.
Composite sub-architecture	A sub-architecture made up of a combination of building blocks of different types.
Continuance goal	A goal that does not require transformations to be attained as it relates to things the organization already does well and wants to continue doing the same way.
Core capability	A capability that provides direct value to customers.
Core function	A function that provides direct value to customers (e.g., Marketing and Sales, Product Development, and Manufacturing).
Current business architecture	The current functioning of the organization. It comprises all of the organization's current business architecture building blocks, their functioning and the relationships they currently have with one another, as well as with the technology asset and natural resource deposit building blocks.

Term	**Definition**
Current enterprise architecture	The current functioning of the organization and its technology assets. It comprises all of the organization's current enterprise architecture building blocks of the organization, their functioning and the relationships they currently have with one another.
Customer value proposition	"The unique mix of product and services attributes, customer relations, and corporate image that a company wants to offer. It defines how the organization will differentiate itself from competitors to attract, retain and deepen relationships with targeted customers" (Kaplan and Norton, 2000, p. 53).
Decision type	A group of decisions that are similar in nature or that pertain to the same subject (e.g., strategy decisions, product design decisions, production planning decisions, customer discount decisions, TBA decisions).
Decomposition relationship	A relationship that exists between two building blocks of the same type when one is a part of the other.
Diagram	"A schematic representation showing the appearance, structure, or workings of something" (*New Oxford American Dictionary*).
Employee value proposition	A set of associations and offerings provided by the organization in return for its employees' work, skills, capabilities and experiences (Minchington, 2010).
Enterprise architecture building block	A business capability, business function, business process, org unit, know-how asset, information asset, brand, natural resource deposit or technology asset.
Formulate and align to strategy (FAS) capability	"A comprehensive and integrated management system that links strategy formulation and planning with operational execution" (Kaplan and Norton 2008, p. 7–8).
Goal	An aim or desired result.
Guideline	A soft constraint that should be followed whenever possible.
Hierarchical relationship	A relationship of either the decomposition or the classification type.
Homogeneous sub-architecture	A sub-architecture made up of building blocks of a particular type.

Term	Definition
Horizontal org unit	A permanent or temporary team that brings together people from one or more vertical org units to facilitate the coordination and decision-making required to achieve particular goals.
Information asset	"Facts provided or learned about something or someone" (*New Oxford American Dictionary*) that the organization possesses.
Initiative	Planned actions undertaken to contribute to one or more goals. An initiative can be a work package, a project or a program.
Intellectual asset	Codified know-how.
Intellectual capital	Tacit know-how with potential value for the organization.
Intellectual property	An intellectual asset that is legally protected by a patent or a copyright.
Know-how asset	Skills and expertise held by the organization and its members.
Long-term financial plan	A long-term forecast of the evolution of the organization's financial position. It describes the organization's financial goals for the next three to five years, when those goals are to be achieved, and the investments that will be needed to reach them. The long-term financial plan includes an income statement, a balance sheet, and a cash flow statement.
Long-term R&D plan	The long-term R&D plan defines what fundamental research, and what products and services development, the organization wants to do, and when, in the coming years. It also identifies the investments that will be needed to execute the plan.
Macro-process	A process made up of lower-level processes.
Mission	An actionable statement that identifies the purpose of the organization. It positions the organization, implicitly or explicitly, in one or more industries and specifies what it aims to do within these industries.
Model	A representation of a given architecture. A model/sub-model represents an architecture/sub-architecture using both building blocks and relationships.

Term	**Definition**
Natural resource deposit	An object such as a parcel of land, natural oil and gas reservoir, ore deposit or forest. A natural resource deposit may become exploitable as a result of the application of scientific knowledge. However, it does not come into existence as a result of such knowledge.
Objective	A measurable, quantified goal with an associated timeframe.
Operating model	The necessary level of business process standardization and integration for delivering goods and services to customers (Ross et al., 2006).
Organizational structure	How the organization's workforce is subdivided into teams (i.e., org units), each of which is headed by a manager and has its own mission. The most visible part of the OS in most organizations is the organizational chart.
Organizational unit (org unit)	A team of people with a common set of goals that is headed by a manager.
Owner value proposition	The value the organization wants to provide for its owners to justify their participation in its ownership.
Partner value proposition	The value the organization provides to its partners (e.g., suppliers, distributors, wholesalers, complementors) – those collaborators that contribute to the organization's customer value proposition – to justify the investments (in time and money) they must make to build and maintain a relationship with the organization.
Peer-to-peer relationship	A relationship between two building blocks that is neither of the decomposition nor of the classification type.
Policy	Explains and describes standards, principles or protocols that all members of an organization must follow. A policy is a hard constraint that members of the organization must abide by.
Position	The place occupied by a person in the organization's vertical organizational structure.
Process	"A set of activities, methods, and practices that transforms a set of inputs into a set of products and services" (Object Management Group, 2008, p. 463)
Process participant	A person, machine or software that performs one or more tasks in a process.

<u>Term</u>	<u>Definition</u>
Program	"A group of related projects, subprograms, and program activities that are managed in a coordinated way to obtain benefits not available from managing them individually" (Project Management Institute, 2008, p. 139).
Project business case	A document that explains the pros and cons of executing the transformations within the scope of a particular project. In addition to determining whether a given project is essential or optional to the implementation of the strategy, a business case should identify the objectives, tangible and intangible benefits, resource requirements (e.g., financial, human, technology and non-technology assets) and risks, and the extended organization's readiness and capacity to execute this project.
Project portfolio	A collection of projects that are grouped together to facilitate the achievement of the selected business objectives (Project Management Institute, 2008).
Project portfolio management	The coordinated management of a project portfolio.
Project team	A temporary org unit set up to create a unique product, service or result.
Project/program charter	A document identifying the purpose and scope of a particular project/program. A charter should identify the project/program sponsor and the set of transformation work packages/projects included in a given project/ program.
Regulation	A rule or directive made and maintained by a government or another authority (Adapted from Oxford American Dictionary).
Result	A deliverable of some kind (e.g., a product manufactured, a service delivered to a customer, a new employee hired, audited financial statements and a project plan).
Result chain	A cognitive map, or "mind map," that graphically represents a shared understanding of what transformations will be undertaken, and in what order, to move the organization towards its target state and achieve its goals (adapted from IT Governance Institute, 2008).

Term	**Definition**
Standard	A rule established by an authority for the measurement of quantity, weight, extent, value, or quality.
Strategic capability	A capability that is key for the organization to be able to deliver on one or more of the four stakeholder value propositions and that the organization has chosen as a means to differentiate itself from its competitors.
Strategy	A market position that an organization adopts to create a unique mix of value for its owners, customers, partners and employees while enabling it to set itself apart from its current and potential competitors in a positive way.
Sub-architecture	A subset of related building blocks that, together with the relationships that link them to one another, form a coherent whole.
Sub-model	A representation of a sub-architecture.
Support capability	A capability that indirectly creates value for customers.
Support function	A function that is necessary for the organization to execute its mission but only indirectly creates value for customers (e.g., Human Resource Management, Financial Resource Management, and Facility Management).
Target	An objective that identifies, at an intermediate point in time, the desired progress towards the attainment of an objective.
Target business architecture	A plan that defines how the organization must function in the future to be able to execute its strategy in full. By "execute its strategy in full," we mean that the organization fully delivers the unique mix of value at the heart of its strategy and that its activities have been transformed accordingly.
Target enterprise architecture	A plan that defines how the organization must function in the future to be able to execute its strategy in full and how the organization's technology assets must function for this purpose. The TEA identifies and defines the desired key features of all the enterprise architecture building blocks (i.e., capabilities, functions, processes, organizational org units, know-how assets, information assets, brands, natural resource deposits and technology assets) and the relationships that all these building blocks will have to have with one another.

Term	Definition
Target information technology enterprise architecture	A plan that defines how the organization's information systems must function in the future to enable the organization to execute its strategy in full.
Target technology architecture	A plan that defines how technologies of a particular type must function in the future to enable the organization to execute its strategy in full.
Task	A piece of work that is done by a single participant.
Technology asset	A tangible or intangible asset that is the result of the application of scientific knowledge for practical purposes.
Transformation goal	A goal that requires transformations to be attained (e.g., build a new factory to increase production).
Transformation plan	A plan that identifies and sequences the transformation projects that the organization must execute during the next three to five years in order to implement parts or all of its target enterprise architecture.
Value	A principle or standard of behavior that is important to the organization.
Vertical org unit	A team of people that results from the hierarchical decomposition of the organization into org units. A vertical org unit has one or more positions associated with it, each of which is occupied by a member of the organization. Typically, one of these positions is that of manager.
View	A particular way of considering or regarding a model/sub-model (adapted from the *New Oxford American Dictionary*).
Vision	A concise inspirational statement that defines the organization's desired long-term state.

Abbreviations

Abbreviation	Meaning
APQC	American Productivity and Quality Center
ARB	Architecture review board
baeFAS	Business-architecture-enabled Formulate and Align to Strategy
BAO	Business architecture office
BCA	Business capability architecture
BCM	Business capability model
BFA	Business function architecture
BFM	Business function model
BIA	Business information architecture
BIM	Business information model
BPA	Business process architecture
BPM	Business process model
BPMN	Business process model & notation
BPMO	Business process management office
BTEP	Business Transformation Enablement Program
BTRA	Business transformation risk analysis
BTRCA	Business transformation readiness and capacity analysis
CBA	Current business architecture
CCO	Chief compliance officer
CEA	Current enterprise architecture
CEO	Chief executive officer
CFO	Chief financial officer
CHRO	Chief human resources officer

Abbreviation	Meaning
CIO	Chief information officer
CMO	Chief marketing officer
CMSO	Change management support office
COO	Chief operating officer
CSO	Chief strategy officer
CVP	Customer value proposition
CxO	Chief x officer
DMAIC	Define, measure, analyze, improve, control
EAIB	Enterprise architecture information base
EAIBMS	Enterprise architecture information base management system
EPMIS	Enterprise performance management information system
EPMO	Enterprise performance management office
EPPMIS	Enterprise project portfolio management information system
ETB	Enterprise transformation board
FAS	Formulate and Align to Strategy
GRC	Governance, risk and compliance
HBAO	Head of the business architecture office
HR	Human resources
IA	Intellectual asset
IC	Intellectual capital
IP	Intellectual property
IT	Information technology
KHA	Know-how architecture
KHM	Know-how model
KPI	Key performance indicator
OA	Organizational architecture
OM	Organization model
OMG	Object Management Group

Abbreviation	**Meaning**
OS	Organizational structure
OSM	Office of strategy management
PCF	Process classification framework
PESTEL	Political, economic, social, technological, environmental, legal
PMI	Project Management Institute
PPM	Project portfolio management
R&D	Research and development
RAPID	Recommend, agree, perform, input, decide
SGB	Strategy governance board
SIPOC	Supplier, input, process, output, customer
SME	Subject matter expert
SWOT	Strengths, weaknesses, opportunities and threats
TBA	Target business architecture
TEA	Target enterprise architecture
TGB	Transformation governance board
TITEA	Target information technology enterprise architecture
TOGAF	The Open Group Architecture Framework
TP	Transformation plan
TPMB	Transformation project management board
TPMO	Transformation project management office
TTA	Target technology architecture

Index

34672996R00143

Printed in Poland
by Amazon Fulfillment
Poland Sp. z o.o., Wrocław